Mothering *Life*

40 day devotional

DEVOTIONS AND REFLECTIONS
FOR POSTPARTUM MOMS

BY: MEREDITH STORRS

TRUTH + LIGHT
by PAPER PEONY PRESS

Mothering Life
Copyright © 2022 Meredith Storrs
Published by Paper Peony Press
San Antonio, TX
www.paperpeonypress.com

ISBN 978-1-961355-01-9

All scripture quotations have been taken from the Christian Standard Bible®, Copyright © 2017 by Holman Bible Publishers. Used by permission. Christian Standard Bible® and CSB® are federally registered trademarks of Holman Bible Publishers.

For bulk, special sales, or ministry purchases, email: reagan@paperpeonypress.com

Author photo © Leslie Kosier

Printed in China.

Contents

To the LA Inklings who have
supported me through many births

Thanks so much for buying our book!
For a free extra, email

paperpeonypress@gmail.com

and we will send something
fun to your inbox!

Welcome

As a mama of three, this is the book I wish I had during those early months with my little ones. Bringing life into the world is such an incredible privilege and joy—and every one of us experiences the journey differently. Motherhood comes with wild highs and complex lows and never ceases to surprise me.

Even with my easiest baby, the brain fog of postpartum made it difficult for me to read more than a few Bible verses at a time. In the isolation and loneliness of lockdown with my pandemic baby, I also longed for a way to process my grief and to find purpose, gratitude, and delight in the midst of trials. With all my children, I wanted to draw near to God, even as I reckoned with my very human limits, and somehow document all the thoughts and feelings I was experiencing. Sleep deprivation, physical healing, and the learning curve of mothering made my usual Bible study routine feel insurmountable.

These short but substantive meditations are designed to meet you in the unique challenges of the postpartum season. There is no prescribed cadence or pace here, so take your time. You might stick with the same verse for a few weeks or even jump ahead or revisit entries as your experience and energy shifts. As we explore the ways God reveals himself through mothering imagery in Scripture, I hope your own story draws you into worship in new ways. Settle in for the snuggles with your baby, and bask in the richness of knowing the good Father who cares for us like the best of mothers.

Your fellow mama and sister,

Meredith

A Note about Diverse Experiences

In this devotional, we will discuss many aspects of motherhood that are distinctly female—pregnancy, labor and delivery, breastfeeding, and more. If you are a mama who has welcomed children into your family without some of these experiences, I know that your heart may be tender to certain topics. My hope is to invite you into an exploration of God's design without adding shame or grief where you already feel like you have missed out. In his good creation, God never meant for one perfect mother to embody his image solo. Each of us will experience different facets of mothering to differing degrees, and it's within the collective diversity of motherhood that we reflect his image more fully. God welcomes us to learn from our own experiences and from one another as we grow in our understanding of his deliverance, nourishment, nearness, and hope.

part 01

Made in His Image

"The same Scripture which speaks in the most exalted way of God's incomparable greatness and majesty, at the same time speaks of Him in figures and images which sparkle with life." —*Herman Bavinck[1]*

We will start our journey together where all of life began—in a garden in the very presence of God. Here we meet our Maker as he was making us and marvel that Eve was able to enjoy him in absolute fullness. The opening chapters of Genesis orient us to our foundational identity as women and now, mothers. God begins his story by showing us how we relate to him and continues revealing more of himself throughout Scripture. In narrative passages, we witness his steadfast character over time. Laws and wisdom literature help us discern between good and bad. And sometimes, God chooses to communicate through poetic comparison. Infused into the world he created is the aroma of the Divine. Scripture invites us to meditate on specific metaphors in the natural world to better understand what God is like. As you ease your mind into spiritual reflection, look around. We are made in his image, and through our experiences with the various elements of motherhood, we will see a glimmer of God.

DATE: / /	BABY IS:	*weeks* | *months old*
I FEEL…		

Stardust

Made in His Image

READ   Genesis 2:7, Philippians 1:6

She was the stuff of stardust, her perfectly round face exploring mine in celestial wonder. A baby. My baby. Somehow made from a bit of me and a bit of him, knit neatly together into glittering eyes and tiny toes. Like the constellations of a planetarium ceiling, nurses danced around the periphery of my birthing room, their movements both slowly melodic and too fast for reality as I tried to comprehend which way was up. My husband and I had just welcomed our first child into the family and with her, the official titles of father and mother for ourselves. We created a life that would change ours forever.

It's a funny thing, really, that the Giver of all life bestows on us the responsibility to replicate it. I'm still getting used to the idea that I—a created thing—was designed as a creator myself. But this is the elemental material of motherhood: to reflect the image and nature of God by creating new life and investing in its flourishing.

In part, mothering is actually how the whole story begins. God speaks life into the darkness of the void, and stars twinkle down upon emergent earth. He lifts humanity out of the dust below, breathing eternity into us. The rest of creation is good, but seated among light and dark, land and sea, flora and fauna, humans are distinct. God creates people out of the basest matter, and yet crowns us to rule the earth as his emissaries. The Creator invites us to join him in the work of forming and filling this earth with life, beauty, and light. He initiates us to parent the created world.

This makes our job as mothers more than a personal life goal, a happy hot mess, or even a heavy burden. The life that comes from within our bodies is a soul with eternal significance and unknowable influence to the world around her. As your baby grows, he will change your perspective on life and grow you in ways unexpected. If you have eyes to see, mothering this child will illuminate the face of God.

As we experience new avenues of mothering, Scripture comes alive in new ways. God has written mothering language into his story to help us know him more deeply. Yes, we know him as our Father, but because he does not exist gendered as we are, he is also like a mother to us. Our growth as mothers is just as much for us as it is for our baby. As she grows, so shall we. And as we learn more about God, his Spirit in us begins to shape-shift our mothering care to look more like his. Our journey as mothers begins with creation, and it never really ends.

When I ponder the story of Genesis, I am struck by how God gives purpose to such an insignificant substance—*dust* becomes *us*. The stuff I usually tread on turns into a vessel for his glory forever. And whatever particles exist out there between the stars are made of the same earth dust as humanity, flung into place by God himself. We are dust, and so is this little baby in your arms. Maybe stardust, blazing a trail of light into eternity.

REFLECT   You have just done an amazing thing—bringing new life into the world. What does it mean to you that God has breathed the breath of life into both you and your baby?

PRAISE   What do you see in your child that inspires awe?

Divine Partnership
Made in His Image

READ   Genesis 1:26–27, Matthew 28:18–20

It still amazes me that God made the universe out of nothing. From snakes that sun on hot desert rocks to the fractals of a purple cauliflower, all of creation proclaims his beauty and majesty from generation to generation. As people, we are the gardeners sent to tend this miracle planet called earth so that God's creation might flourish. God designed us to reflect his image collectively as we partner with him to bring goodness to the world. But how do we learn what he is like so that we can follow the calling he designed for us?

Throughout Scripture, God shares the answer to this question through stories. The history of Israel, God's chosen people, demonstrates how much he loves and pursues us. He also reveals his nature to us in the Bible through recurring themes and imagery to help the ideas stick. God is a good King whose rule is marked by protection and care for our well-being. God is a good Shepherd who guides us in the way we should go. God is a good Father who cherishes his children. And as he teaches us the way of wisdom, our Father God also demonstrates what it looks like to be a good mother. God is neither male nor female, and his vocation is not limited to grazing fields or regal courts. Yet each of these analogies offers us a partial view of our incomprehensible God.

We get to know God by meditating on his stories, comparing and contrasting him with the human kings, shepherds, and fathers and mothers of the Bible. If you happen to be a shepherd, then stories about sheep will be meaningful to you in a way that a university professor won't really comprehend. The same is true when we read passages in the Bible where God talks about breastfeeding, birthing, and midwifery. Our own experiences as mothers add richness to our understanding of God. When we have endured the difficulty of labor, related passages light up on the page in a new way. As our understanding of God grows, so too does our understanding of the job of a mother. God made us like him, and he wants all women—even those who do not birth children of their own—to join in his work of spiritually mothering the world and all its creatures. He invites us to actively use our unique gifts within our specific circumstances to make the world a more beautiful place.

All Christians are united in this call to promote flourishing, and God equips men and women with diverse abilities that coordinate together for the task of making disciples. Today, this means caring for the new life God has placed in your family. As your baby grows, God himself will cherish her, sometimes through your mothering care and sometimes more directly as your baby's ultimate life-giver. Raising our babies is a partnership between us and a spouse, us and our community. But it goes deeper. Motherhood is a partnership with God to further the work he has planned in our baby's life.

Purple cauliflower was never found in the vegetable gardens of Eden. It emerged from the work of careful crossbreeding and natural mutations over time,[2] a prime example of divine-human partnership. We enjoy this colorful produce in our crudités today because some of our ancestors made new plants out of the raw materials God gave them. He invites us into a similar work, to labor with our circumstances, personal gifting, and raw material, and to watch the fractals grow.

REFLECT What does it mean to you that you are made in God's image?

PRAISE How has God brought goodness into your world this week?

Made to Be Fruitful

Made in His Image

READ   Genesis 1:28–31, James 1:17–18

The summer after I got married, I accomplished two fairly unimpressive tasks. I was recently unemployed, and so between looking for work and trying to make myself useful around the apartment, I grew the most expensive tomatoes of my life and read all seven *Harry Potter* books. While I filled my mind with the magical tales of enduring friendship and triumph over evil, I filled a pot on the porch in our courtyard with seed, soil, and water.

Reading is a favorite fuel of mine. I love to get lost in a whimsical story as much as I enjoy someone's graduate dissertation. From simple but profound poetry to well-researched journalism, I like peeking through windows into other worlds and discovering kernels of truth. In a way, reading functions like food for our minds. What we take in affects what we put back out.

As with all the ways we fuel our mind and body, some foods are more life-giving than others—and context matters. Sometimes we really need a protein-dense meal with leafy greens to boost energy and make sure it all comes out smoothly on the other end. Other times, savoring a rich confection draws us to worship the Giver of sweet blessings. We might be fueled by lively conversation one day and need solitude and rest on another. Contemplating the themes of a film might give life and so might listening to an old hymn.

So how can we tell what would be most filling from day to day, hour to hour? We look for fruit.

In the Garden, God called Adam and Eve to be fruitful and multiply. The physical fruitfulness of raising children would be important for their work in ruling and ordering the world, but before they could accomplish either of those things, they needed fuel. And God gave generously—not only by supplying a multitude of plants to enjoy but by offering his very presence. God provided them food for the body and food for the soul so that out of their fullness, they could bear fruit.

Especially in the season of young motherhood, fruitfulness can be hard to see. We have to keep fueling ourselves and our babies even when there is no evidence of growth (or the growth that we would like) . . . yet.

This is where wisdom comes in. The conventional wisdom of generations of farmers tells us that plants need sun, soil, and water to grow. We listen to advice about plants in the same way that we listen to advice about mothering. There will always be new tips and tricks, modern methods for infusing nutrients into soil, and state-of-the-art gadgets that promise to regulate water distribution—but the principles are the same. So, too, with mothering. Behind the barrage of internet recommendations and ads for the latest mommy must-haves, we evaluate contemporary methods against sage principles. Does this product help me take care of my body? Will this app keep me connected to my community? What might help me clear a little brain fog to soak in the Word of God?

In the early years of motherhood, when fruit is hard to see, we can trust that orienting ourselves around Scripture will always mean growth. It might not look how we expect, but we trek on, following God's directions for life because he designed how it should operate.

My horticultural ambitions that newlywed summer were an abject failure. I didn't have enough sunlight for my tomatoes, so after all the investment of pot and fertilizer and trellis, I harvested two small, dense, thick-skinned tomatoes. But where my green thumb may have failed me, God did not. Instead of tomatoes, other fruit grew. Reading grew my imagination and empathy, while job hunting stretched my endurance and faith. God sustained me in a number of ways through this season of uncertainty because he was the source of everything I really needed—light and food and shelter, all in one.

REFLECT   What does fueling yourself look like in this postpartum season? How might you humbly ask for support?

PRAISE   Even one good newborn feeding is worth celebrating. Take a moment to thank God for even the smallest success.

Made Wonderfully
Made in His Image

READ   Psalm 139:13–16, Ephesians 2:10, Proverbs 3:11–12

When I was a senior in high school, I took Floral Design as an elective course because, well, these are the kinds of electives you can take at a public school in Texas. I still remember a few of the principles of arrangement and how I overused birds-of-paradise in all my designs, but my most distinct memory was of the two boys who sat at the back of the class hacking at flowers and hoping not to flunk. These teens were members of the Future Farmers of America, an organization that encourages youth to compete in a number of agricultural contests, from raising animals to growing crops. In order to stay eligible for competitions in the FFA, a student needed to be enrolled in one of the agriculture classes offered at my school.

These boys—let's call them Matt and Kyle—wore Wranglers unironically, and while I sometimes donned my mom's vintage cowboy boots as a fashion statement, their mud-caked Justins were built for true labor. Matt and Kyle's floral arrangements left much to be desired, but these boys' hearts were beautiful. Here they were, two rough-and-tumble young men, scraping a couple of Cs in the only remaining elective that would allow them to do the thing they truly wanted to do. In so many ways, they were unlike me, but I remember them fondly because Matt and Kyle knew exactly who they were and what they loved. They pursued their passions relentlessly.

When God makes us in his image, he does not carbon copy. The Psalms remind us that we are wondrously made, each of us beautiful in her own way. And just like shards of a mirror, each of us reflects God in different ways, from different angles. For one, it's passion for justice that propelled her to study law. For another, a gentle caregiving spirit inspired work with the autistic community. Some of us lift paintbrushes in worship, and others faithfully serve meal after meal despite tired feet or thankless customers. None of us is wonderful in just one way—we are an elaborate bouquet of God's fragrance, meant to share his goodness throughout the world.

Sometimes I get a little tripped up by the idea that God has prepared good works for me to walk in. What if I'm on the wrong path? What if he made me with all these good gifts to use, and I squander them? These pressures often run through my mind. God has given me so much, and I want to show him that I deserve it, or at least that I will wield the gifts responsibly. But when God blesses people in Scripture, it's never a gift with a catch. He doesn't wag his finger and remind us to stay in line. Instead, his Word is replete with examples of God's unending love. He cares for us dearly as children, and even his discipline is for our good.

I love sharing with friends when I see God's goodness reflected in them. I marvel when I see it in myself. But with each new generation, his light lives on. Every baby we bear is a fresh reminder that God arranges us wonderfully. And the paths we each will walk can supply flourishing to the world in different ways. Even if they require a detour through an unusual elective along the way.

REFLECT Where do you see glimpses of God's nature in yourself? In your baby?

PRAISE Thank God for a way that his discipline or instruction has blessed you.

Broken Spirits
Made in His Image

READ   Proverbs 17:22, Genesis 3:16–19

Sometimes my mothering journey feels more wandering than wonderful. When a birth plan didn't go the way I'd hoped or the postpartum season offered unwelcome changes to my body and personal autonomy, I became discouraged, fearful, and sometimes even a little angry. Now, as I enter each new stage of motherhood, my view of the world often becomes obscured by thorns and thistles, and the labor is hard in the wilderness.

Inside my head, faithful mentors' voices echo a directive that is sometimes tossed around in Christian circles—"Lay your burdens at the foot of the cross." And I wonder, where exactly do I go in order to do that? Can I find the latest Bible story movie set and act my way into the ancient Near East? If I go into a dark closet or to the highest point in the city or if I stare long enough into the ocean, will I be able to find Jesus there? Where is my enchanted mirror? *Show me the face of the Lord.*

Each time a baby is born, we celebrate God's wonderful design. But we do so outside of the perfect rest and communion of life in the Garden of Eden. Everything after Genesis 3—our lives included—is marked with all kinds of suffering. We lament alongside the mothers of Scripture every time a child gets sick, or our bodies fail, or a plan falls through, or a person lets us down. We are not the first generation to struggle as mothers, and our grief is echoed in the stories of Scripture. We watch in horror as Pharaoh throws baby boys into the Nile and Herod slaughters the innocents. Our mourning is matched in Job and Naomi. We see our hurt reflected in the eyes of the abused woman in Judges, and we wail alongside the Psalms' composers. We sit in shock as

Joseph is carted away by slave traders, a victim of his own brothers. We think of his mother Rachel who endured a life of competition and conflict with her sister that was sadly repeated among their sons.

The Bible is full of grief upon grief. And yet we still approach it as a redemption story. We scour these tragic moments of Scripture looking for hints of the Messiah to come. We remember the promise God gave to Eve, and we rejoice when Jesus crushes the serpent's head. Because it's not just our struggles and sadness that we see mirrored in these pages. The Bible is where we can stare full into the wonderful goodness of God.

A broken spirit is crushed under the weight of her laments. But God invites us to unburden our hearts in prayer and clear the brambles from view. By sharing our honest grief with God directly, we acknowledge the full weight of sin and suffering that only He can redeem. We do not need to deny our suffering to find redemption because Jesus has already embraced the ultimate suffering in order to redeem us. We draw near to the source of all life to feel his warmth on our faces, trusting that he will attend our labors. This is joy—to wail with the ancients and still hunt expectantly for signs of the Son.

REFLECT   The early weeks with a new baby are notoriously emotional. In what ways has your labor been painful? How might lamenting your struggle lead to hope?

PRAISE   What detail of your pregnancy or birth makes your heart joyful?

Our Need for Rest

Made in His Image

READ   Matthew 11:28–30, Psalm 127:1–2

I make a point to never offer advice about sleep or potty training. No one is allowed to be good at everything, and these two subjects are among my gravest deficiencies. By the grace of God, I bumbled my way through, and my kids all eventually made it out of diapers and (mostly) sleep through the night nowadays. Helping children learn to sleep particularly put me through the ringer. It required me to give up my basic human need for rest in order to help a tiny person whose needs conflicted with my own. Yes, I have grown perseverance in this area over the years. And, if I ever have time to myself, I usually choose to nap.

Sleep is one of the hot-button topics featured in the never-ending parade of parenting books. Motherhood has more supposed "rights" and "wrongs" than a home decor influencer's bed has pillows. We often fear that making the wrong choices about food or sleep or discipline will doom our children to a lesser experience of life. If it's not caring for their basic needs that trips you up, maybe it's spiritual instruction, cultural competence, school choice, mindfulness, grit, socialization, or the Internet, oh my! Not only do we feel pressure to research all the best ways to raise a child, we expect to have superhuman capacity to accomplish everything we've read about, despite any hurdles or challenging circumstances along the way. We think that only those who can manage to check every box will have perfect, happy children. This is evidence that motherhood has become our religion, and unlike the way of Jesus, the yoke is heavy.

By contrast, the gospel message does not burden us with senseless rituals or require a perfect score card. Jesus's death and resurrection make it possible for us to be called children of God. We parent as those who are dearly loved by our own heavenly parent. Rather than hustle to guarantee the success of our children, we humbly point them to our source of hope. This is a huge relief, because if I had to defy failure for their sake, then my children would be doomed before they even left the womb.

As humans, our bodies are designed to require about eight hours of sleep every day in order to function properly. This need for rest is a daily reminder that we are not all-powerful, all-knowing creatures. We are not designed to be gods over our own lives. We need rest, and by the grace of God we can actually take the rest we need. We are able to lay our heads confidently on the pillow each night (maybe just one stuffed with down or 34 in different shapes and sizes if that's your thing) because we don't have to hold the world together. God cares for our children more than we ever could. We can trust him with their future—even in our missteps—because our perfection doesn't save our children. His perfection does. His promise of rest goes beyond our physical need for a power nap—Jesus releases us from the burden of perfection. Our souls can rest from the hustle, starting each new day with whatever sleep baby permits.

REFLECT Has sleep deprivation set in? In what ways do you need support for physical rest? What areas of control can you prayerfully release in order to experience soul-level rest?

PRAISE What is one area in your mothering that is coming more naturally or where you are seeing some personal growth?

Life Gestates

Made in His Image

And it always seems that just when daily life seems most unbearable, stretching out before me like a prison sentence, when I seem most dead inside, reduced to mindlessness, bitter tears or both, that what is inmost breaks forth, and I realize that what had seemed "dead time" was actually a period of gestation.

—Kathleen Norris[3]

READ   Lamentations 3:22–26

___

The doldrums are a place along the equator where ships get stuck with no wind.[4] We sometimes use this term to describe our own emotional malaise or seasons of life when monotony rules. For me, this was most palpable during the final weeks of pregnancy, as I found myself waiting for the wind to finally catch my sails—for aches and pains to give way to real contractions, progress, and proof of life.

Pregnancy is such a strange season because the visible changes are so gradual. A swelling belly hides so much of the miracle happening underneath, as the mother experiencing gestation feels its deep effects. Since others cannot see the visible product, especially in the early weeks, we often struggle to feel as though our fatigue is justified. Nearly all of us have wondered why our normal daily functions become so difficult to accomplish. *Where did I put down my tea? Why am I falling asleep at 8 p.m.? What's the word for those things I hang on the wall by the . . . other thing I need? Am I getting dumber?* It may not look like we are running a marathon, but these symptoms are akin to the cramps, chafing, and dehydration that athletes experience during a long race. They are evidence of the grueling work of growing a new human.

Our spiritual life follows a similar pattern. Sometimes we see tangible answers to our prayers, children sharing with a friend something we had recently taught them, or our sacrificial effort manifesting in community impact. But so much of life is just getting up each morning, doing the task in front of us, and hoping that it all comes out ok in the end. Many of our days are filled with normal routines and honest hard work rather than exciting twists and turns.

And when nothing is happening, we start to wonder if something might be dying. *Have I lost my edge? Is all the time and energy I invest in my children really worth it?*

But lack of wind does not indicate a problem with the ship itself. A personal dry spell might be a wake-up call to intervene before you veer too far off course, but it could just as easily be God's way of slowing you down to savor a moment, or grow a new skill, or rest and repair. Motherhood will have its fair share of labor, so if your current season is quiet, lean into the preparation. Trust the promise of Lamentations, that God's good mercies will fill your sail again someday soon.

REFLECT   What does it mean to you that God's mercies never end?

PRAISE   In what ways has God shown his faithful love to you, even if you are experiencing a period of emotional or spiritual "gestation"?

part 02

God Delivers Us from Death and Destruction

Genesis reveals God as our Creator, the source of all life. He defines what motherhood should be because he designed it, and we will find the greatest peace and joy in creating new life when we follow his lead. As we continue our exploration through the Bible, we will discover imagery about wombs, labor, birth, and midwifery. God calls himself our Deliverer, and while we might be used to hearing this word in the context of delivering nations or individuals from duress, we will see the intimacy of God's deliverance in the mothering language he employs.

DATE: / /	BABY IS:	weeks | months old
I FEEL...		

God Is Like a Midwife

God Delivers Us from Death and Destruction

READ   Isaiah 66:9–11

For most of human history, childbirth was exclusively the realm of women. Once the signs of early labor gave into a regular cadence of contractions, the family would send for the village midwife or an older, experienced woman nearby. The mother's nearest female friends and relatives gathered behind closed doors to support her birth. Young girls learned about labor as they brought fresh rags and warm water in and out of the delivery room. Before there were hospitals, epidurals, C-sections, and beds with stirrups and collapsible ends, birth happened in the home, on a stool, surrounded by other women, with the expert guidance of a midwife.

These days, our support team during birth might look very different. Maybe your husband or mother was able to attend, or you hired the expertise of a doula or birth coach. Most of us, having never helped our aunties or family friends give birth, take classes and watch videos to better understand what labor will be like. We rely on doctors and nurses and incredible benefits of technology that have plummeted the infant and maternal mortality rate. These are good gifts.

But for the earliest readers of Scripture, comparisons of God to our deliverer are visceral. Yes, sometimes God's deliverance looks like parting seas and slaying giants. But sometimes his deliverance looks more like the intimacy of a midwife, rescuing us from bleeding out in sin-stained circumstances. This is more than a sentimental image of God patting our hand and whispering, "You can do it!" as we sweat and push. I do believe he is with us always, including during those precarious moments of birth. But for those who have seen the inside of a birthing room, the image of God as a midwife is raw and messy. God draws near to us in our most vulnerable moments. Like a midwife, he is intimately aware of how our bodies are designed to work. We follow his guidance through all the trials of life when he tells us to shift our weight this way or push right in this moment and not a moment before. His touch can relax our tense muscles with the strength of affirming presence, and he wisely guides us in the way we ought to move.

An earthly midwife must war against the physical constraints of our fragile humanity—placenta previa, a breech baby, prolapse of the umbilical cord, or any number of other life-threatening complications. She relies on training, wisdom, and quite a lot of common grace to deliver new life. God attends our birth as well. He is present with us as we bring babies into the world, but his work also encompasses the spiritual birth and deliverance that is part of our continual renewal as his children. We can trust him to bring forth new spiritual life even in the messiest circumstances, even in those moments when we fear we are past the point of no return. He intervenes. He transforms even the ugliest pain and deepest disappointments. As the Savior who died laboring on our behalf, he delivers again and again in the perfect power of one who burst forth from the womb of the earth, resurrected, whole, and forever alive.

The support and deliverance of a midwife is intimate, gently massaging new life into the world with poise and wisdom. Her work is like God's work, close and comforting, but also death-defying.

REFLECT   How does your own birth experience illuminate the way you read the passage in Isaiah? How does the promise of God bringing new life give you comfort when plans go awry?

PRAISE   Praise God for ways that you have seen his deliverance.

A Life-Giving Womb
God Delivers Us from Death and Destruction

READ   Job 38:8–11, 25–30

Maybe it was the faulty wirings of a still-developing adolescent brain, but I didn't connect menstruation to the act of creating life until after I was married. Periods meant blood in my underwear and figuring out how to use a tampon by fumbling my way through the line-drawn instructions in the box. At best, it was a monthly inconvenience, and at worst, it meant a few days on the couch clutching my mom's 1970s floral print heating pad. To my teenage mind, periods were somehow disembodied from my womb.

When God confronts Job about God's sovereignty and authority over all the world, he asks a number of poetic, rhetorical questions. They are meant to lead Job to recognize that God is the source and master of all creation, which he formed out of nothing and controls according to his good design and pleasure. In this line of questioning, God incorporates both fathering and mothering imagery, not to suggest literal conception or birth, but to present a window into the kind of life-giving Creator he is. God describes elements of creation as if they were bursting forth from his own womb, the sea and ice and frost emerging out of the depths of himself like a crowning baby. God draws our attention to birth and motherhood, showcasing how his authority is deeply integrated with his life-giving capacity. He made the world and rules over it, but not as an authoritarian dictator who strips the land of all its resources. He rules as a mother who longs to see the life he created grow and flourish toward maturity.

Having a womb is intrinsic to womanhood and points to God's creative capacity. Even those of us who never bear our own biological children will walk through life with a reminder in our inmost being of God's creative capacity. Nearly all of us will experience the hormonal ebbs and surges that come with this life-giving ability. Each month, we bleed because we have not conceived, and the blood we shed signals a kind of death. Blood means that my body prepared for new life, but for any number of reasons, did not receive it this month.

Just like spring flowers that break through cold, dead earth, uterine glands stretch open again every month, releasing life-sustaining fluid and multiplying the blood vessels to rebuild the uterine lining.[5] Women's bodies are so intent on making new life that they keep repeating this cycle even when we prefer they wouldn't. Even when we are grieved that they haven't conceived. Our bodies try to get pregnant roughly every twenty-eight days—that's hundreds of attempts during the reproductive years of a woman today.

Still, conception is not a given, a truth many women experience quite painfully during struggles with fertility or prolonged seasons of singleness. If we are blessed to conceive, the fruitfulness of our wombs is still precarious. We lose sweet babies before ever feeling the pleasure of plump cheeks on our chest. Our God, who has watched the destruction and decay of the world he created, is deeply attuned to our pain in these moments. But as our bodies quietly work away to reproduce each month, they testify to God's promise that full and final rebirth is coming. The One who created this world also controls its future—a future that will break the cycle of death, offering life forevermore.

REFLECT   How do you feel about having a womb? In what ways does your current experience color the way you think about God's relationship to creation? How does God's power over his creation differ from your own influence as a mother?

PRAISE   A God with the kind of power described in the book of Job would be terrifying if he were not loving and just. What other attributes of God are you glad work in tandem?

God Embraces Labor
God Delivers Us from Death and Destruction

"If our picture of strength is a laboring woman, then strength entails enduring, receiving help and support, being open to pain and risk . . . .Strength even entails giving yourself over to the possibility of death."

—Lauren Winner[6]

READ   Isaiah 42:14–16, Romans 8:26–27

I think I might have done it wrong. Pregnancy. Birth. Parenting. The transitional kindergarten program for my daughter. The haircut for my son. Worries about my choices and aptitude as a mother regularly sneak through the confident exterior I project, dancing wildly in my gut. Motherhood reminds me so often of my weakness that I sometimes forget the ways it is making me strong.

When God compares himself to a laboring woman, his description is raw and guttural. Some translations of today's passage in Isaiah even use words like "cry out" or "pant"[7] to describe the intensity and exasperation that laboring women experience. My own and others' birth stories remind me that bringing forth life is uniquely vulnerable. So many of us are plagued with feelings of inadequacy, even in the midst of near transcendent experiences. Laboring women often engage with surging contractions instinctually, making bestial sounds to accompany animalistic motion. We can lose all sense of modesty, space, and time, desperately requiring the support and protection of others even as we access untapped strength for the final push. Labor is vulnerable, but it is not weak.

The lead-up to labor through pregnancy is also hard on our bodies. Growing a human life requires increased nutrients, and if you aren't able to eat the additional vitamins that the baby needs, she will strip them straight from your own bones. If you manage to live through childbirth, keeping your new baby fed requires more calories than pregnancy. Breastfeeding may be natural, but it is an endeavor with a painful and steep learning curve, and so too is mothering this tiny new creation. We have no guarantee that we will get to see our babies grow up or walk in the way of the Lord. All of that hard work for the very real chance of great grief and loss.

So the fact that labor itself pushes women to the brink of our capacity, causing us to groan inexpressibly, seems fitting. During labor, we face our vulnerability dead on. Birthing a child requires our whole self in a way that few other experiences in life do—every scrap of our attention, every muscle in our body, every gulp of air in our lungs. Paradoxically, labor also displays our strength. In giving everything we have to this vulnerable task, we showcase a fortitude to endure pain for a purpose, as well as our willingness, like Christ, to lay down our own life if it is required. Labor prepares us for motherhood, where even in our weakness, the Lord is strong.

The God who labored to deliver Israel from exile is laboring even now. God compares his desire for redemption with that of a laboring woman, moaning and deep breathing through the pain at hand, ready to lay waste to any enemy that would threaten the child she so dearly loves. God makes himself vulnerable even to the point of death on a cross so that we might truly live.

REFLECT   What does God's choice to become vulnerable to death teach you about his character? Think about your own experience with the vulnerability and strength of birth. How does it inform your view of the Holy Spirit's work in our hearts?

PRAISE   In what ways is God helping you in your weaknesses as a mother?

The Birth of Wisdom
God Delivers Us from Death and Destruction

READ   Proverbs 8:22–31, Genesis 4:1, Hebrews 1:1–3

The most entertaining part of teaching Sunday school is snack time. I especially enjoy preschoolers because they are quite communicative and also wildly unfiltered. As we sit around lily pad-shaped tables, munching on gluten-free pretzels and grouping gummies by color, I like to ask them questions about life. *What is your teacher like? What do you play with your friends at school? What did you do for mommy today for Mother's Day?* The answer to the last question is overwhelmingly similar year after year—"We made her COFFEE!" Mothers of preschoolers, it turns out, need lots of caffeine.

My conversations with four-year-olds can be comically revealing. Older children eventually learn some discretion, and teens might quit paying attention altogether, but the littles are so delightfully fresh. They observe us in our best and worst, and when they aren't explicitly sharing our secrets, they are mimicking our behavior, trying their best to grow into the model of humanity set before them. In both intentional and accidental ways, we make little people in our own image.

In the book of Proverbs, we read a poetic account of wisdom personified as a woman, bearing the image of God just like one of the kids in my Sunday school class. We are encouraged to seek after her like a young man seeks a wife, and to live according to her teaching and example. Lady Wisdom, as she is sometimes called, reminds us that following the law of God is more valuable than gold or jewels. She reminds us to act with shrewdness and discretion. And she tells us in vivid metaphor that she is intimately aware of the best way to live because she was with God when he created the world.

She knows how God has designed us and can guide our flourishing.

Lady Wisdom describes her own origin using the language of childbirth. When she claims that the Lord "acquired" her, she employs the same Hebrew word that Eve used to describe birthing her firstborn, Cain.[8] The parallel between these two passages points to God as the source of Wisdom and invites us not only to look back at Genesis but also forward to Christ. The author of Hebrews opens his letter by explaining that God made the whole universe in beautiful trinitarian unity with Jesus, the Son. While Lady Wisdom invites us to follow her in a more poetic sense, Jesus is the very wisdom of God made flesh, able to demonstrate more concretely the nature of God that Lady Wisdom has been describing.

When we look at our own children, we might notice dad's dimples or grandma's eyes. Children bear the markings of those whose DNA replicates within their cells. They are made of us and become even more like us through constant interaction during the early years. In the poetry of Proverbs and the life of Christ himself we get an insider's view of what God is like. The Son of God knows his ways. He has learned the difference between good and bad directly from the source. He thinks and speaks and acts like him. And if we follow his footsteps, we will too.

REFLECT   How have you grown in wisdom since becoming a mom? What does pursuing wisdom look like for you with your current limitations?

PRAISE   God reveals his wisdom through Scripture and also in the context of our spiritual communities. Thank God for those who have shown you an example of wisdom.

Born of the Spirit

God Delivers Us from Death and Destruction

READ   John 3:5–8

Blue jays grow up and fly from their nest. Chimpanzees swing from tree to tree. Jellyfish pulse along ocean currents. A raccoon prowls at night. Every creature God made has a specific form that is related to its function, and each is most fulfilled doing what it was made to do. A fish out of water cannot thrive, nor can a bird on the seafloor.

While the circumstances of our birth don't dictate everything about the person we will become, being born a human takes a few options off the table. Our bodies operate a certain way and when we use them as God designed, life will go more smoothly. At the most basic level, we cannot survive unless we follow a few rules—eat, sleep, find shelter. We don't last long underwater. And if we want to move from place to place, we can either walk or invent a form of faster transportation.

We also learn in Scripture that our souls thrive when we follow God's way of living. A healthy body is wired to send cues to keep ourselves healthy. We are born with the impulse to seek food and sleep (even if it takes some training from mom to regulate this), but for our *spirit* to seek what is good, we must be born again.

Longtime Christians are so familiar with this idea of being "born again" that we typically gloss over the way Jesus describes our rebirth—it's the Holy Spirit who gives birth to our new spirit. And because Father, Son, and Spirit are one, this means a Christian rebirth comes from God himself. We are God's brand new spiritual babies. As humans, we were already born physically reflecting the image of God, each of us a mirror fragment showcasing God's form and function. But once reborn in spirit, Christians are indwelled by God himself. Now, our new spirit is most satisfied when we move and speak and think like him.

The blue jay cannot see the wind that lifts him into flight, but he feels it flex his feathers. Christians similarly grow in sensitivity to the Holy Spirit. We learn what it feels like to lean into his guidance. We begin to trust that he will take us where we need to go. As children spiritually birthed of God, our heart, mind, and body come into better alignment now that our spirit is renewed. Of course this does not miraculously repair every broken part of our lives. We continue to sin and to suffer in a world that is not really home. But on the inside, our form and function are no longer at odds. Where we once wandered aimlessly, we can see in the dark. Where we held our breath hopelessly, we are lifted out of the water. New spirits help us to quit chasing a way of living that defied our original design. Spiritual rebirth doesn't change us from mongoose to mouse; it unlocks how we were meant to operate all along. It animates our creatureliness in all the right ways, offering not only the awareness for how to live rightly but the capacity to choose it as well.

REFLECT   What has it felt like to watch your little one physically grow? What has this taught you about spiritual growth? What does it look like to be sensitive to the "wind" of the Holy Spirit, even if you do not know where it is blowing?

PRAISE   Thank God for ways he has changed your heart since your spiritual rebirth.

Jesus Births New Life

God Delivers Us from Death and Destruction

READ   John 17:1–5, John 19:33–34, John 10:10

Eighteen hours passed between my water breaking and the first call I made to my OB. She was not pleased. I had taken a natural childbirth class and wanted very badly to labor at home as long as possible. The problem was, my contractions still hadn't started, despite the circus of tricks I'd tried, and my doctor worried that allowing my daughter to stay in utero much longer might put both of us at risk for infection. My hour had come—whether I was ready or not—and I would soon welcome my baby into the world.

Two thousand years ago in a garden called Gethsemane, Jesus used the same common birthing phrase, "the hour has come," to describe his journey to the cross.[9] His work was a different kind of labor that would end in death, but also, miraculously, new life.

Before childbirth comes the labor pains. And so if we view Jesus's final hours on earth in parallel with the experience of labor, we might imagine Jesus as he is praying in the garden, feeling the anguish of the work ahead of him, like the twinge of a pregnant woman's early irregular contractions. He knows the work his body must do, but it is still daunting to stand at the beginning of the journey. Jesus willingly entered into the laborious work of the cross for us, and after hours of excruciating pain, after his final breath, a Roman soldier pierced his side. Blood and water trickled down the legs of our life-giving God.

Medical professionals who have studied the effects of crucifixion on the body suggest that the soldier's spear pierced Jesus's lungs and heart, which would have been surrounded by a buildup of fluid typical in cases of asphyxiation.[10]

And while there is great meditative weight to the idea that Jesus's death struck straight to the heart, I cannot help but see in this rupture of blood and water a similarity to the laboring woman whose amniotic sac is pierced in order to make labor go faster and aid the transition to pushing. This is the final tense moment, where it appears to the watching disciples that everything is coming undone. In the vulnerability of Jesus's death, the whole plan seems exposed, risking the spread of infecting doubt. But the pushing and crowning and emerging forth to new life—it was just moments away.

God doesn't give spiritual birth to us like a frog or fish, casually dropping several thousand eggs. God labors to make us new. He sweats and groans and bleeds. His crucifixion looked chaotic and frightening to his confused followers. But God knew exactly how it would turn out. And just as a woman's labor must always come to its conclusion, whether ending in life or death, Jesus saw his work on the cross to completion. In the end, the grave did not have the final say. Birth did.

REFLECT   In what ways do you see connections between the labor of childbirth and Jesus's work in your life? How does comparing labor with the crucifixion enhance your understanding of its intensity and purpose?

PRAISE   Eternal life is not just forever in length but forever in scope. In what ways have you experienced abundance as a mother?

A Community of Midwives
God Delivers Us from Death and Destruction

READ   Psalm 22:9–10, Exodus 1:8–21

In my imagination, the villages of the ancient Near East, with their multigenerational homes and tribal faithfulness, provided all the warm and loving community I often long for. I live far from my blood relatives and though I've been lovingly surrounded by a church community, I've also felt the deep loneliness that comes with our modern, Western home structure, where nuclear families live in isolated boxes, separated by obstacles like traffic and postindustrial work schedules. In the hours I spent pumping milk behind a bathroom partition, I sometimes wondered what it would have been like to gather around the quern to grind grain with other mamas, able to follow the natural rhythms of my baby's hunger instead of marking myself unavailable in measured intervals on my Google calendar. The simplicity of village life seemed superior. Never mind the lack of running water or absence of a deep freezer full of ice cream . . .

The opening of the Exodus story reminds me that every generation of women has had nuanced struggles in their mothering. In addition to the differences in technology and medicine, women throughout history have experienced war, oppression, family trauma, and pandemics. The women in Exodus may have lived in more communal household structures, but that doesn't mean they could always avoid loneliness as mothers. Instead of problem solving how to fit their Mommy and Me group around a nap schedule, they had to navigate raising children in the context of their own enslavement. And yet as Pharaoh continued to heavily oppress their families, the Hebrew women exploded with children. Their community grew, guided and supported by the midwives Shiphrah and Puah.

The text hints to us that these midwives were originally childless. Only after defying Pharaoh's edict to kill all the baby boys does God bless them with children. These two barren women, looking beyond their own loneliness and possible shame, support a nation of women who by all practical measures should be too starved and overworked to carry their babies to term. But by divine intervention, these women carry on.

Our triune God is one, yet exists in the perfect communion of three persons. He brings forth all of creation and attends our spiritual rebirth with a deliverance that is communal. He exemplifies the kind of community we should build as mothers, while also promising to never leave us abandoned in a world where birth plans cannot be perfect. Shiphrah and Puah, like all good midwives, did not simply catch babies and hand them off with a hope and a prayer. They were integrated into a community trying to faithfully raise the next generation to follow God. Their midwifery invites us to reflect on the ways God delivers us securely into our new spiritual family.

God's work does not expire after the placenta has passed and our uterus contracts back down to size. He invites us into the community of his family—which we'll talk about more in the closing entries of this book—and ensures that we are secure in his arms. But for now, heads nestled near the heartbeat of our God who brings life to all, we will find more than comfort. Because after the labor is over, he nurses us to grow.

REFLECT   Psalm 22 describes God like a midwife who becomes our adoptive mother. How do these two images inform your sense of security and your place in the family of God? When was the last time you connected with your community (and should the answer be "today")?

PRAISE   Who in your community has been your birth support, both in tangible and spiritual ways?

part 03

God Nourishes Us from His Own Body

The God of the Bible does not deliver his people only to abandon them later to fend for themselves. He goes with us into wild places and provides for our needs. Just as our babies need nourishment to survive and thrive, we also need God to sustain us. And he nourishes those who depend on him.

DATE: / /	BABY IS:	weeks | months old
I FEEL...		

Bread and Water

God Nourishes Us from His Own Body

READ   John 6:32–35, John 4:13–14, 1 Corinthians 11:23–26

Making milk is costly for a mother. Between the calories she needs to eat, cracked nipples, blocked ducts, and myriad other roadblocks that mamas experience when trying to feed their babies, it's no wonder that so many children in ancient times didn't make it past infancy. Today, we have a number of support systems that help us feed newborns when challenges arise— lactation consultants, access to formula, and the whole of the internet that can answer our questions at the simple bidding of Siri or Alexa. Still, I've met precious few mothers who say that feeding their infants was a piece of cake.

Jesus himself lays the table for our understanding of a God who nourishes us—he is the bread of life, a spring of water that won't run dry. In the coming pages, we will consider several passages that speak directly about breastfeeding and milk, but I want to start with Jesus because his teaching about our nourishment is central to the Christian life. We remember his death and resurrection with the practice of communion, crushing bread between our teeth as we think of his body broken for us. Tasting the wine, we consider his blood poured out, as we are allowed to drink deeply from the well of everlasting life and be satisfied. Salvation is expressed as food.

If this sounds a little cannibalistic, you wouldn't be the first to raise an eyebrow. The early church faced some scrutiny based on the Roman misunderstanding of their communion practices,[11] but the body and blood are not literal. Jesus's teaching about bread and wine invites us to meditate on the relationship between God's provision and the food we eat every day. The ceremony of communion recalls Jesus's last supper with the disciples, which also should remind us about the first Passover in Egypt and the gift of manna in the wilderness. The bread and wine are a metaphor proclaiming the good news of Christ's death and resurrection. Just as we need food and water to live, we need God to sustain us, and he does this by offering his own body for the task.

Both men and women know what it feels like to work and sacrifice for a child. Fathers can give time, energy, and resources just as much as mothers do. But a mother shares her body with a child in an extraordinary way that men will never experience. She shares her womb as baby's first home, and she sustains her child with milk. Jesus also comes to earth ready to share his body, willing to feed and sustain us no matter the cost. He teaches often about bread, wine, and water so that we might know his goodness in tangible ways. On the cross, we see Jesus give his body over to death so that we might live, but in his teaching, he speaks of *living* water and the bread of *life*, not dead flesh. Truly, Jesus is the Lamb of God, slain for us, drawing us near to be nourished.

REFLECT   In what ways does your need for food help you better understand your need for Jesus? What can you do this week to ensure that you are not spiritually starving?

PRAISE   How has God spiritually sustained you in recent weeks?

Letdown

God Nourishes Us from His Own Body

READ   Isaiah 49:15

I have my share of nursing horror stories—engorgement, undiagnosed tongue-tie, weeping through cracked nipples during middle-of-the-night feedings, pumping in strange spaces, and one dramatic 2 a.m. trip to the ER. But retrospect has been generous to me, and mostly, when I think about breastfeeding, I remember the full-body exhale that came when my milk let down for a properly latched baby. On the best of days, we settled in for a snuggle among a perfectly supportive pile of pillows. I was satisfied watching my satisfied little one.

In the book of Isaiah, God compares himself to a nursing mother to show us how deeply moved he is to care for us. He employs an absurd rhetorical question, "Can a woman forget her nursing child?" to help us see that he will never forget or forsake us. This is just one of many passages in Scripture that nod to our relationship as God's children and the deep affection he feels for us. This correlation is more than sentimentality, though. By highlighting the specific experience of nursing, God articulates his nearness in starkly physical terms.

Letdown is the prickling sensation that a woman experiences when her milk begins to flow. Women's bodies are not made like a beer tap—pull the lever and fill a glass whenever you feel a little parched. Instead, a mother's breasts replenish milk on a cycle, about every three to four hours when our babies are newborn. As her baby grows older, the breastfeeding mother's body learns the rhythms of his feeding schedule and adjusts to refill on cue. Usually, the letdown reflex is triggered once a baby begins to suck, but it can also happen in response to visual cues, thoughts, or simply time of day. It's preposterous to imagine that a nursing mama would forget her baby because if she waited too long to feed him, the sensation of milk filling her breasts would be a tangible, undeniable reminder.

Similarly, God knows our needs in a way that defies understanding. God does not have a body, so we don't come from a physical womb or nurse at actual breasts. And yet in Scripture, he employs the language of our own bodily experience as mothers to reveal his character to us. God tells Isaiah that whenever we feel like God might have forgotten about us, we should think about a young mother leaking milk at the distant sound of a baby's cry. His connection to us is even stronger than that. The inexplicable bodily reactions that we might experience in relation to our own children are just a shadow of his deep, abiding love for us, a love that is more than a thought exercise or serene emotional high. The God who provides us nourishment as his children gives his whole self to the task. And he is satisfied to satisfy us.

REFLECT How does your experience feeding your child—whether you are breastfeeding, pumping, or preparing formula—impact the way that you understand Isaiah's rhetorical question? How has motherhood shaped your view of God's faithfulness?

PRAISE What does it mean to you that God will not forget you?

Milk Dries Up
God Nourishes Us from His Own Body

READ   Psalm 104:24–28, Numbers 11:11–15

The day I knew my last child was about to wean, I took a video of myself to document this closing chapter. Pregnancy and birth were harder for me to manage. Nursing was precious.

Friends of mine have had a range of experiences transitioning to motherhood. Some felt magical and glowing throughout pregnancy, while others spent months on bed rest. A few could tell you every milk-producing tea, herb, and cookie recipe in existence (and whether or not any of them made a lick of difference). I know women who made so much milk they could donate the extra, women who couldn't conceive and adopted instead, and women who labored for less than an hour. One of my favorite anecdotes is of a mama who reached down at just the right moment to catch her firstborn with her own two hands. I think of her every time I read the nativity story and wonder if Mary had a similarly powerful experience.

In every era and across the world, women are burdened by a number of cultural ideals related to their capacity to bear children. For most of human history, childbirth was central to a woman's identity, and societies were structured to support this work. In some ways, this has been a beautiful gift, making space for women to do the important work of caregiving that their bodies are uniquely suited to do. But in a world filled with sin and suffering, this has also come with unrealistic expectations, stereotypes, pressures to conform, and a narrow definition of success.

When our milk dries up, whether it came too early or much later than we'd hoped, our children move on to new forms of nourishment. Each of us will have a spectrum of emotions about this transition and a different set of challenges with every new stage of feeding. In the book of Numbers, Moses can relate. He cries out to God in frustration, comparing his leadership to the experience of a mother with too many mouths to feed. He is overwhelmed by his inability to provide for the people and ready to wholesale quit.

We work to feed our children—first milk, then solid food. And like Moses, we might feel at times like we are not up to the task. But God is able to step in where we are unable. He can sustain us during the years when we are physically sustaining babies with our own milk, and he will also provide for us during the seasons when kids seem to suck everything else right out of us. Because his nourishment can never run dry, he has enough for us and enough for our children too. He gives us what we need at just the right time, even if we, like Moses, are not sure that we believe it.

The early church father Augustine once suggested that we might see a picture of grace in the gift of milk from mother to baby. Yes, a mother works hard to create the environment for healthy feeding, learning alongside her baby how to breastfeed, and yet she is unable to actually make the milk flow. Her milk-producing body is a free gift, designed brilliantly by God to function as it does.[12] If we are able to nurse, it is not because of any good thing we have done, but a free gift of God. And when we are no longer able, grace—and maybe a video or two—remains.

REFLECT   What are you learning about God's sustaining grace? Does this impact the pressure you feel as a mother, either with feeding or in another area? In what ways can you relate to Moses's lament?

PRAISE   When has God shown up to give you nourishment at just the right time?

Personalized Spiritual Milk
God Nourishes Us from His Own Body

READ   Psalm 34:8–10, John 1:1–3, 1 Peter 2:2–3,
Hebrews 4:12

In the early years after my third baby was born, my creativity with dinner plummeted. I'm the kind of Southern girl who always prided herself in offering someone another helping. (Heaven forbid anyone left my table hungry.) Even in college, I found it important to own a casserole warmer. But between two picky big kids, a long commute, and the toddler pulling on my pant leg, I lost some of my culinary spark. Dinners got random. We were abundantly fortunate to have access to fresh ingredients, but I had very little capacity to plan out recipes or even appropriately pair mains and sides. So sometimes dinner was leftover meatloaf, a can of beans, and grapes. Or I might dish up the crumbles at the end of the pita chip bag if the kids just couldn't stomach the fact that the couscous was *mixed* with vegetables. No one went hungry, though, so I still count it as a win.

I frequently tell my kids that food has two purposes—fuel and pleasure. God gives us food to sustain our bodies and also to enjoy. We eat some foods primarily for fuel and some primarily to taste and see that the Lord is good. Often, food can serve both roles. Dinner together as a family is an opportunity for us to praise the God who provides nourishment and to delight in the sweetness of his good creation. Even on days when the options are lackluster.

The apostle Peter offers a poignant analogy for anyone who has seen a young mother with her child. Christians, he argues, are like newborns, and the Bible is the milk we crave. This is not because ink on papyrus can fill our bellies. Scripture is more than words on a page; it is God himself breathed out through stories and explicit guidance. Reading our Bible is like drinking milk straight from the source.

Breast milk has a pretty miraculous design. A woman's breasts can actually take cues from her baby's saliva to adjust the composition of her milk based on the child's needs.[13] And while the words in our Bible do not rearrange themselves for our particular questions and struggles, Scripture is still living and active in our lives through the work of the Holy Spirit. I can read the same passage at ages 12 and 20 and 68 and learn new things about God each time, not by my own doing, but because God's Spirit personally feeds the words to me. Through prayer and meditation, the Holy Spirit helps us understand the Bible and apply what we are reading to our specific circumstances. Reading the Bible in this way allows us to drink in the tailor-made nourishment of God.

When we feast on Scripture, we experience the best kind of food, a meal made for all of us collectively and for each of us personally. It is fuel to sustain us in this life and abundant pleasure forevermore.

REFLECT What are some of the ways that reading the Bible fuels you? In what other ways do you taste the goodness of the Lord?

PRAISE What passage of Scripture feels personal, like it was written just to sustain you?

Planting Seeds

God Nourishes Us from His Own Body

READ   Galatians 6:9, 1 Corinthians 3:6–7

The closest I've come to reaping crops (besides the aforementioned tomato fiasco) was the summer we gleaned corn from a family friend's farm. These fields were part of a research plot at Texas A&M University, and in this particular year, an entire field of sweet corn was reserved for employees to enjoy. The harvest was so abundant that Mr. Collins encouraged us to pick as much as we could carry.

We went to the fields in the cool of the morning, but during late summer in Texas, "cool" meant that the temperature was at least 85 degrees by 8 a.m. We sweat through the long pants and shirts required to protect our skin from sharp stalks, but the misery of the sun melted away once we were back on the porch shucking and sampling several trash bags' worth of sweet corn. It was divine.

The Bible often speaks about harvest, and I ruminate on what that means as a parent. Every day we till soil and plant, tending our little crops on their way to maturity, and on the days when the heat is especially fierce, I pray for the harvest to be full and sweet like Mr. Collins' corn. I'm still in the middle years with my own kids so I don't expect it anytime soon. But even my empty nester friends talk as if they are still tending the fields. We are all seed planters, faithfully watering and nurturing our vulnerable little sprouts with hopes of savoring the fruit of our labor in the cool of a shaded porch someday.

As parents, we know that the time invested in our children will shape the adults they become. We don't want to understate our importance, lest we off-load their discipleship to outside influences. At the same time, the entirety of their growth doesn't actually rest on our shoulders. We plant. We water. But God is the one who does the growing. We fill our kids' bellies, but the God who knit them together in our womb is in control of the bodily systems that make their limbs get longer. We fill their minds with Scripture, but only the Holy Spirit can morph their hearts to love like he does. What amazes me about God's nourishment for his children is that he is both the sacrificial giver of food and the one who converts intake into output. He grows the bodies that he feeds.

Or put another way, God controls the harvest. He can call forth abundance from our meager seed offerings because even though we are invited into the planting, God has more than enough food to spare. We are welcomed to feast at his banquet table. The skills and gifts we bring into our parenting have great value, but they also do not make or break the meal.

It's ok if some parts of motherhood make you feel like you were *made for this*, and other parts make you wonder if you are missing the right genes for farming. Every day that you show up for your child—to feed her, to clothe him, to snuggle—this is all very good work. Each act of love is a seed planted in the hearts of our dear ones, and they are never wasted.

REFLECT How does an understanding of harvest impact your attitude toward mothering today? What encouragement from Scripture might help you persevere when the sun is bearing down?

PRAISE Look at how much your baby has grown! Praise God for new milestones.

Satisfied

God Nourishes Us from His Own Body

"A mother holds her baby eight inches from her face, and looks into their big baby eyes, and sustains them with her own life ... this is what God says he is like, but even better."

—*Carissa Quinn*[14]

READ   Hosea 11:3–4

When you are awake at 4 a.m. for your third feeding of the night, the phrase "sleeping like a baby" makes about as much sense to you as liquid pajamas or a levitating car seat. Somehow this expression persists even though newborns rarely sleep for long, undisturbed periods. I've mentioned before that we don't manage sleep very well in my household, but during the early months of nursing my babies, I did consistently marvel at the relationship between drinking milk and falling into a blissful slumber.

Maybe you have seen this happen. Your baby loses her latch, lips pursing for a couple more phantom sucks. She takes one shuttering sigh and drifts into peaceful dreams with the satisfied look that some have jokingly called "milk drunk." If this is what people mean by "sleeping like a baby," then sign me up.

A recently fed baby in his mother's arms can rest peacefully because he feels safe and satisfied. He is sustained by the food from his life-giver and also protected within her arms. Night after night, mothers around the world are moved by compassion for their vulnerable babies and shake off their own sleep to continue nourishing.

The God we worship is compassionate like a mother. In fact, the Hebrew word for compassion is related to the word for womb. So, when Scripture speaks of God's compassion, it evokes the emotional attachment and commitment of a mother. God is moved from his inward being not only to care for us as children, but to act on our behalf.[15] God sacrifices to feed us, and only in him can we be fully satisfied.

Of all the places in the Bible where God describes Israel as his children, Hosea chapter 11 is the most tender. The NIV translation of verse 4 employs the image of a mother caressing her child cheek to cheek, and as I read it, I can almost feel that baby softness on my own face. My toddler's squishy features are starting to give way to the toned musculature of the active little boy he is becoming. At night though, when he floats off to sleep on the ocean waves of his sound machine, his face softens. I lean down just as I used to after he finished nursing and hold my cheek to his. I take in his smell and pray that he will learn to trust Christ with the same reckless abandon that he gives to his own flawed but faithful mother. His satisfaction with me is a beautiful picture of the satisfaction God offers to all of us. We only need to sigh deeply and rest in his arms.

REFLECT   How has your understanding of compassion changed since becoming a mother? How is your caregiving similar to and also different from the way God cares for you? What does your baby's satisfaction after a feeding teach you about being satisfied in the Lord?

PRAISE   In what ways has God been tender with you?

Comfort Food

God Nourishes Us from His Own Body

READ   Isaiah 66:12–13, Isaiah 41:10

According to family lore, my first word was "casserole." This seems implausible based on my limited understanding of language formation, but it does make for a great story. According to my parents, my brother, disgusted by dinner one night, asked, "Ew gross, what is that?" And so they explained that they were serving a casserole, which is a catch-all term for a number of melty, baked, single-dish recipes. Blank stare. "Cass-er-ole" they repeated a few more times, slowing down so that my brother could hear and process each syllable. Knowing the word for this pan full of mixed cream, rice, and mushy vegetables didn't seem to resolve his disgust, but in the silence that followed, I pointed to and named the food that my brother would not.

Once I learned enough about cooking to work without a recipe, I discovered that roasted fresh vegetables and a homemade basic white sauce really leveled up my casserole game, introducing textures and flavor that couldn't be matched by canned cream soup. Some might call this sacrilege, but I have been quite pleased with the balance between my current tastes and the comfort of a dish I have presumably loved since infancy. Meanwhile, others in my household today will respectfully pass on casserole, no matter how precisely balanced the flavor profile. But for me, even a modified version of this comfort food serves its purpose. Certain cooking just tastes like home.

God's comfort is like a home-cooked meal. He is the bread of life, nourishing us from his own body, and the food he offers can warm our soul like mac and cheese, fried rice, chicken curry, pad Thai, poutine, goulash, beef stew, apple pie—fill in the blank. When God invites us to taste and see that he is good, the food he provides is comforting because it reminds us of home.

Isaiah 66 personifies Zion, the promised land, as a baby-wearing, nursing mama. Not only will she carry Israel on her hip, close to her heart, but she will also bounce her child delightedly on her lap. God wants his people to see that in the land he provides for them, they will find nourishment, nearness, and the wholehearted joy of a playing child. Like a mother, God offers the comfort and safety of his presence. We are able to rest and play because our home with him is warm, inviting, and healthy. This home is a safe place to share in his presence now, and it is also secure for us forevermore.

Our relationship to food today isn't always a source of peace. We might struggle with nutritional challenges, emotional eating, food insecurity, or other effects of the Fall. These very real, very painful challenges might threaten to obstruct our view of a nourishing God. We can't wipe these problems away like crumbs on the counter from last night's dinner. But all hope is not lost. God is like a mother who invites us to draw near to him, where he can begin to mend and heal our longing hearts.

REFLECT What is the relationship between nourishment and comfort in your life? How is this impacted by a God-centered idea of nourishment? How does the imagery in Isaiah 66 influence your understanding of God's comfort?

PRAISE Thank God for ways he has recently been a comfort in your mothering journey.

part 04

God Nurtures Us Close to His Heart

God demonstrates a kind of mothering that knows and meets our deepest needs. In our families, we bring babies into the world and sustain them with our own bodies, but we also recognize that their needs are more than physical. God's mothering care is holistic, enveloping us in a sense of safety, comfort, emotional attachment, guidance, and more.

DATE: / /	BABY IS:	weeks | months old
I FEEL...		

God as a Mother Hen

God Nurtures Us Close to His Heart

"Let not the thought of the hen leave your mind, who with her drooping feathers covers her tender brood and with broken sound calls her peeping chicks to her side, while those that turn away from her caressing wings, in their pride, become the prey of hawks."

—Augustine[16]

READ   Matthew 23:37, Isaiah 40:11

The best hens I've known were stage managers. To be fair, everything I understand about poultry I've gathered from a couple of school field trips, childhood stories, and a movie or two, so perhaps I am lacking in personal references. I am aware that comparing women to chickens is usually meant as an insult, evoking the inane clucking of a bunch of old biddies. But when the Bible references birds, they are often discussed within object lessons about home and provision. When I read about Jesus's longing to gather Israel like a hen gathers chicks under her wings, I am reminded of these friends of mine. They knew how to envelop me in the kind of hug that felt like all my problems would melt away.

A stage manager's job is not maternal by nature, though. It requires precise attention to detail and a level of coordination that would shame a synchronized swim team. Shadowing the director throughout a play's rehearsals, the stage manager carefully notes where each actor is supposed to go on stage and communicates between all the technical and design departments to ensure that every aspect of the production stays unified and on task. When it's time for the curtain to open, she is clad in black on a headset, cueing each sound effect and projection so that they land exactly as they should. If the show goes on, it's because she held all the pieces together.

It's one thing to enjoy the embrace of a particularly warm and cuddly mother figure. It's an altogether more powerful experience to be held by someone who seems like she can command the constellations. After all, motherhood is more than hugs and back rubs. A mother who only comforts but never disciplines, encourages, or advocates is no better than a soft blanket and a teddy bear—satisfying for a moment, but lacking any real capacity to solve the problem that drove us to seek relief in the first place. In the motherly embrace of God, we experience the balance of warmth and power that provides both comfort and true help.

I can only guess what baby chicks feel in the crook of their mother's wing, but my fortunate encounters with hen-like women must come pretty close. Their love pours out in a protective presence made all the more rich by their ability to solve problems and also put me back in line when needed. They invite us to see that God's parental love is more than the duty of child support or the empty promise of some future outing to the zoo. Our mothering God draws us near, nurturing us under his wing in an embrace that really can heal old wounds—because unlike even the most incredible stage manager, he actually did hang the moon.

REFLECT What would it look like for you to allow God to nurture you like a mother hen? How do the words in Isaiah color your understanding of God's nurturing? What personal experiences or ideas might impact your willingness to be close to him?

PRAISE In what ways does the combination of God's warmth and power comfort you?

A Nature of Attachment

God Nurtures Us Close to His Heart

READ   Psalm 17:8, Psalm 57:1

Something remarkable happens to a mother's brain during pregnancy, birth, and the early stages of caregiving. Nerve junctions actually rewire as she develops an attachment to her infant. These new pathways refine her nurturing skill set, hard-coding a bond between mother and child that is measurable on an MRI.[17] Brain changes like these are part of a complex life stage coined in the 1970s as "matrescence," in which both biological and adoptive mothers experience radical shifts in their physical, emotional, and relational lives as they learn to care for themselves and their babies at the same time.[18] Similar to adolescence, the road to motherhood involves its own growth spurts, where some days can feel hopeless and disconnected, even while God is working under the surface strengthening muscles we never knew we had.

Whether or not you feel it at this moment, God has designed within you an instinctive desire to hold your baby close, to feed and love and protect him. We are born with this capacity and develop it in the context of healthy relationships as we mature. In early motherhood, as you traverse the wild mountains of matrescence, this nurturing capacity kicks into high gear as your brain reprograms to nurture your new baby.*

Human reflex is another incredible aspect of our design. Our hearts beat automatically. Our lungs fill with air. We blink when something splashes in our eyes. Our brain sends warning signals in the form of spiked anxiety when we perceive that danger is near. If attacked, we might curl into a ball to protect our most vulnerable organs. All human bodies perform a number of functions like these, without our minds willing them to happen. During matrescence, mothers grow a new set of instincts as their bodies change and their experience deepens. We might wake more easily to baby's cries or react more quickly to catch a tripping toddler. Our deep-seated impulse to care for our child eventually manifests in reflex-like behavior.

The psalmist relies on our understanding of instinct and reflex when he poetically calls for God to respond as a mother to us. Long before Jesus identified himself with a mother hen, the Psalms incorporated imagery of seeking refuge under the wing of God. Psalm 17 pairs God's desire to offer refuge with the reflex we experience to guard our eyes against an incoming foreign object.

Psalms is the largest book in the Bible. This songbook is a biblical worship manual, showing us how to pray, lament, and celebrate. The Psalms are raw and honest, but they are not an arbitrary mess of emotion and desire. When the psalmist makes an appeal to God, he asks for a response that aligns with God's character, expectantly imploring him to keep his promises. In fact, the idea of seeking refuge with God appears over forty times in these songs.[19] The psalmist asks God to draw us under his wing because he believes that God will do it. He trusts that God feels an even more perfect attachment to us than a mother feels to her child.

Deeper than human DNA is God's compulsion to care for his vulnerable children. It is in his nature to nurture us. As mothers, we will struggle with attachment in varying degrees with each of our own children. But when we sense a deep draw toward caregiving, we can celebrate God's image reflected in us. And when it seems like our bodies don't have the right reflexes, we can remember that we too are children, invited to seek refuge and learn from a mother whose wiring works just perfectly.

> **A note on personal experience:** *When trauma or difficult circumstances impede the natural process of attachment, mothers need and deserve support. If you are currently experiencing more severe struggles with the transition to motherhood, please reach out to your doctor, a therapist or counselor, or your church community. God does not ask us to walk these roads alone.*

REFLECT What feels like a reflex or instinct for you in your mothering? What are some ways to seek refuge in God when you feel your strength or wisdom are not enough?

PRAISE In what ways have you felt the blessing of natural bonding with your baby?

Protection

God Nurtures Us Close to His Heart

READ   Psalm 91:1–6, Deuteronomy 31:6

I gave myself a lot of grace with cleaning when we moved into our new, nearly one-hundred-year-old house. Between its original cracks and all the new ones we made as we renovated, dust and bits of drywall powder were a regular feature. One evening while I worked late into the night, I glimpsed a long, stringy dust bunny fluttering in the shadows of the fireplace logs. I deliberately ignored it, turning back to the design edits I was ticking off my to-do list one by one. Vacuuming would be tomorrow's problem. But when the dust curled worm-like from left to right, it pulled my full attention. Dust bunnies roll or float askew as one piece. They don't swipe like a curvy windshield wiper. However, a mouse tail does.

Slowly and cautiously, I dipped my head around the side of the screen to confirm my suspicion and then did what any reasonable woman would do at nearly midnight—I called my husband's cell phone, woke him out of a dead sleep, and pleaded with him to come rescue me. Most of the time I am grown-up and independent enough to take care of myself, but in this case, I wanted protection. And my husband couldn't effectively protect me from a distance.

Just before Israel enters the promised land, the nation's leadership transfers from Moses to Joshua, and three times in the same chapter, God reminds Joshua of his nearness. Twice God promises not to leave or abandon Joshua, no matter how fierce their enemy may seem. Then, when God foretells that his own people will turn away, he concludes by reiterating the same encouragement—*Be strong. I am with you.* God protects Joshua from enemies on the outside. And when the rebellion comes from within, God remains steadfast.

As we care for the little chickies under our wings, enemies more fierce than my fireplace mouse invade from all directions. Whether it's a hostile neighbor or an unwelcoming climate, we will find a number of challenges that war against the good mothering work we are trying to accomplish. School presents ideas that conflict with our values. Siblings have it out for each other (and know all the right buttons to press). City planners seem blissfully unaware that families might live here too. Even in the best of circumstances, time betrays us, stretching on when we wish it wouldn't and then evaporating all too soon.

As mothers, we can be strong in the face of our enemies, whether they be open aggressors or persistent inconveniences. We guard against these outside influences, while also recognizing that sin sprouts up in the hearts of our own children and ourselves too. In these moments, God whispers the same refrain to us as he did to Joshua. *Be strong. I am with you.*

God describes his protection using more than just battle imagery. Great warriors go out into battle. They lead the charge and are first to put their safety on the line, even as they call others to fight alongside them. Commanders slay and obliterate. They guard the castle by going out to keep its borders secure. It's hard to imagine a military leader discarding his breastplate in the mudroom at the end of the day and curling up with a brood of children for his nightly rendition of *Goodnight Moon.* And yet God suggests he looks after us in both of these ways. He transcends our understanding of fatherly and motherly attributes, encompassing them both.

Elsewhere, God describes himself as our defender, but in Psalm 91 he claims to be the fortress itself. Here again, he invites us to take refuge under his wing. His protection is complete in a way that we rarely see exemplified on earth, both going out to battle and also drawing us into his nurturing embrace. God does not promise that our bodies will remain safe and unharmed from the effects of sin in the world, but he is regularly generous in his care. Those who trust in him find peace beyond understanding because they know their souls are safely guarded for eternity, where moth, rust, and mouse cannot destroy.

REFLECT   What "enemies" are you facing today? What attributes of God's character inspire you to courageously protect your child? What would it look like to lay down your fears?

PRAISE   How has God graciously protected you and baby in this season?

Loss

God Nurtures Us Close to His Heart

READ   Psalm 34:17–18, 73:23–28, 30:4–5

My first baby was due in June. My husband and I went together to our first appointment, marveled at the lovely pulsing heartbeat on the screen, and shared our joy with friends and family. Then, at nearly 20 weeks pregnant and full with Thanksgiving turkey, I went to my OB for a routine checkup. She used an audio device that couldn't get the right angle on my belly to find the baby's heartbeat again. Two days later, in a cold room alone, the unfamiliar faces of the ultrasound technicians shared that my baby stopped growing at about 12 weeks. The heart that beat so strongly in that early appointment had likely stopped around that time.

I don't know how I got the words out when I phoned my husband from the now-vacant examination room, but he left his office and was driving to meet me before the call was over. In the interim, I talked with my mother, who passed along the words that my late grandfather, an incredibly kind and wise physician, once told her after she also experienced a miscarriage: "God knows when a baby isn't healthy, and sometimes he graciously brings them home." People might say any number of trite or unhelpful things when you lose a child, and perhaps these words would fall in that category for some. But I heard them in the voice of my Pappaw, delivered with the comfort of the wry old man who brought me ice cream for breakfast in bed when I stayed over at his house as a child. The words had a sense of place, spoken by a person whose nearness represented security and peace.

Knowing the *why* for our suffering doesn't always take away the pain. But for me, thinking about *where* was a source of comfort. I could never hold the babies I lost, but God does. I wouldn't get to bring them into my own home, but God brought them into his. They would experience God's own care from their earliest moments, drawn into his nurturing presence, a place where I also desperately needed to be.

At home, our tears flowed as my husband and I sat on the couch considering this deep sorrow. At a loss for our own words, we opened an old hymnal. We felt broken before God, but we sang our pain through the words of faithful Christians in ages past and trusted that the Lord would hear us.

The Psalms rejoice in God's nearness, protection, and care. They also lament. They give voice to our pain and gently hold our hand, guiding us to God's presence for comfort. When a baby cries or a child skins his knee, a mother's embrace can quiet the tears. Kisses have healing power for stubbed toes and bumped heads. Our children instinctively come to us for comfort because in their world, we are the biggest, most capable companion. Because they have learned to trust our nurturing when sailing is smooth, we are the safest place through rough waters. Moms can turn sobs into giggles.

God's mothering care is balm to the brokenhearted because he draws us near. Just as we could not nurture our children properly from a distance, God is close in times of defeat, affliction, impatience, *and* joy. His nurturing is unlimited in scope and available to all who would reach out and take his hand.

REFLECT   How has God ministered to you when your spirit was crushed? What do you need to cry out about today?

PRAISE   God does not require us to plaster smiles over hurting hearts. Take some time to thank God that he hears your laments.

Comparison

God Nurtures Us Close to His Heart

READ   1 Thessalonians 2:7–8, Hebrews 12:1–2,
1 Corinthians 11:1

No one raises children in a vacuum, and for this I am thankful. Try as I might to be "mom enough" for my babies, I truly need our village. Not only is my human capacity limited, but my own unique skills and gifting mean I'm more successful in certain areas of mothering than others. I rely on my spiritual family to be legs and ears and elbows, members of this body that work together with me in my parenting journey. Many of these influences are atmospheric—musical appreciation picked up on a playdate, or another set of hands to throw around the football when our community group gathers—but some people play a more integral role. One of these people in our family is Miss Cindy. My third calls her "my Cinny," an attempt to say her name that morphs into an accidental (yet insightfully appropriate) possessive. Miss Cindy has played an important caregiving role for all three of my children, and I cherish the bond my son has with her. She has taught him colors and numbers and can turn a painted handprint into basically anything. She mothers alongside me, caring for my son as one of her own.

Paul, who famously urged the Corinthian church to follow him as he followed Christ, describes a caregiving relationship between himself and the churches he planted using the same nurturing imagery that we've seen God employ. In his letter to the Thessalonians, he compares himself to a wet nurse, whose profession is to feed and raise another's children. But the phrase he uses is of a nurse caring for her own children,[20] suggesting that the relationship he has with this community blurs the line between professional and personal. He is tender toward the spiritual needs of the church, bonded in the powerful way that a nursing woman is to those she feeds.

Leadership in the Kingdom of God must incorporate the nurturing presence of mothers. Women are gentle, connected, and caring in meaningful ways that help us understand God's character. Certainly, a great deal of nuance exists in how many women express these traits, and both men and women will see some overlap between their skills. Even Paul, a church father figure, draws on feminine themes to describe his own leadership and partners with women like Priscilla, Phoebe, and Junia in his collaborative ministry work. In Scripture, God invites diverse personalities to work together to build up the church. From Deborah to David, Hannah to John the Baptist, the great cloud of witnesses in Scripture testify to God's inclusion. He delights to call and empower even the seemingly weakest among us. Together in community, together with him, we humbly disciple the next generation.

When we compare ourselves to other moms, we often look through the lens of lack. We focus on our failures and their talent, skill, beauty, and access. What if instead we saw them as our fellow spiritual mamas and considered what each of us offers as a caregiver in the family of God? All of our gifts, from the spiritual to the more mundane, are given in service to build up the church. So if we are to compare, let us do it in celebration. Our whole village thrives when our babies enjoy the nurturing care of different members of the community.

REFLECT   How might you celebrate the successes of other moms? What special gifts do you have to share with your community?

PRAISE   How do various strengths in women you know highlight attributes of God in unique ways?

Mother Bird

God Nurtures Us Close to His Heart

READ   John 1:1–13

My Mammaw had a voice like butterscotch candy. I loved climbing into her lap with a book, listening to her slow, southern drawl coat every word. A favorite selection of mine was P. D. Eastman's classic, *Are You My Mother?* In this story a baby bird wakes one morning to find his mother missing. He traverses the countryside asking a dog, a cow, and even a bucket truck if they are his mother. Each one is like him in some ways, but only his mother, once he finally finds her, reflects his identity in fullness.

I grew up with a gaggle of aunties and older women, who taught me all sorts of important lady things—how to braid hair into an updo and sit up straight with my ankles crossed. They also taught me about the Bible. I learned to study Scripture deeply and to seek wisdom from older Christians. When I moved to Los Angeles for college, my first goal was to find a church and some church ladies. Instead, I found that in a city where everyone is young (or at least works hard to look the part), finding an older woman to invest in my development felt like a knockoff of Eastman's book. *Are you my mentor?* Sisters became essential, and together we fought to point each other back to God's word.

Sunday school taught me that God, through his Spirit, would grow me to look more like Christ. I could look to the example of Jesus to find abundant guidance about navigating the world in light of God's design and values. But this still left me wondering about my role as a woman. How could a single, male Jesus demonstrate godly womanhood, let alone motherhood? If I wanted to understand my own identity as a mother, I would need to find the one

I'm modeled after. To chase down this question, I dug deep into the stories of the women in Scripture, where I found examples of bravery, faith, and community impact, even in spite of their imperfections. Still, these excellent mentors couldn't quite answer my original question.

But God could.

God is neither male nor female, yet he designed our sexed differences to reflect aspects of his nature to the world. As he engages with humanity, trying to help us understand what he is like, he uses the language of mothering to give a glimpse into his character. In this way, God also reveals for us what kind of mothering is reflective of him. We ask, *Are you my mother?* But God sees the question behind the question. He knows how our hearts long for an example to follow as we raise our children. We are looking for a mother bird, and he answers, *I am the one you are looking for.*

The gospel writer John tells us that Jesus is God and was with God in the beginning, creating alongside his Father. God's words spoke our universe into existence many years before he would enter into it as the Word made flesh. The gift of God's word, the Bible, is a gift of self. Within its pages God reveals what he is like—not a hen or a dog or a plane or a Snort—but like the mother bird, our source, example, and comfort.

REFLECT   What have you learned from mentors and women in Scripture about being a good mother? What questions still linger for you? How might God illuminate your understanding of motherhood?

PRAISE   How has God been a light in the darkness for you?

Coming Out of the Fog
God Nurtures Us Close to His Heart

READ   Genesis 1:2–3, Deuteronomy 32:11–18

What's your best baby brain story? Have you lost keys or phone or wallet, only to discover them a day later beneath a bag of edamame in the freezer? Wrapped an end-of-day team meeting before you realized that your shirt was inside out? Perhaps you've had such a bad bout of morning sickness that you legitimately feared you might vomit out the baby. Or cried in desperation because punching the number again and again into your computer keyboard just wouldn't make the phone work.

The exhaustion of pregnancy and the postpartum period can definitely mess with your head, but even in the silliest of brain fog faux pas, I have yet to meet a mother whose pregnancy or birth caused her to forget her identity entirely. Even after a night of seemingly endless feedings, most of us could still recite where we live now and where we moved from. Managing the multitasking required during motherhood might make us a touch forgetful, but we still know who to call sister and auntie and mom.

One of Moses's final speeches to the nation of Israel employs a lot of the imagery we have considered so far—a God who births, nourishes, and spreads his wings over us. But the warmth of these images is juxtaposed with a warning. We, like the nation of Israel, are prone to forget and rebel.

Balancing a family's demands can stretch the most capable of women to her snapping point. It's easy to get busy with arranging schedules, resetting play spaces, and supplying yet another round of clothes for those ever-lengthening arms and legs. We know that time with God is important. We are profoundly grateful that he invites us to draw near. And we also hit snooze six times before escaping from our latest nightmare about accidentally walking naked into our high school Geometry class.

In the beginning of creation, God's own Spirit hovered over the dark, watery depths just like the eagle in Moses's song who hovers over its young. God's first creative act was to bring forth light. Sometimes when our family life feels formless and void, light is precisely what we need. Before we can make and enjoy good things, we must be able to see rightly.

Jesus, the Light of the World, shows us the way we should walk. He is our model while we do this good and challenging work of mothering. He is the shepherd who celebrates at the return of a single lost sheep, the mother who hovers over her nest, and he is also the parent who scans the horizon, ready with a banquet if his prodigal daughter would just return. We may be simply lost in a bit of brain fog or we might have strayed so far that we no longer remember the warmth of God's embrace, but he does not forget us. The porch light is on. All we have to do is come back home.

REFLECT   How might your family or community support you during times that you find it difficult to draw near to God? What reminders of his goodness can you incorporate into your daily life?

PRAISE   How do you respond to God's nurturing care? What imagery from today's passage in Deuteronomy leads you to thanksgiving?

part 05

God Makes a Home for Us

Our nurturing God is the consummate homemaker. He has been designing spaces for his people since the dawn of time and promises to dwell with us through his Holy Spirit forevermore. As we tour through some of the homes that God has made, we will notice patterns that should shape our own aesthetic. His homemaking sets the tone for our own.

DATE: / /	BABY IS:	_weeks_ | _months old_
I FEEL...		

Making a Home in Eden
God Makes a Home for Us

READ   Revelation 21:1–6, 22–25, Psalm 119:105

It doesn't matter how many home renovation shows I watch, one of the most challenging design elements for me to visualize is the interplay of color and light within a space. I know conceptually that lighting matters. Thousands of shades of paint must exist for some intentional reason. But for the life of me, I cannot light or paint a room inside my head. I have to see it to believe it.

Fortunately, my husband's mind projects in vivid detail. This means that while I am perusing bedding, furniture, or appliances, he can imagine these items arranged in a space and offer the optimal color swatches given the tone of the floor and how the light will shift throughout the day. I didn't really appreciate the beauty of all this until I finally gave in on painting our bedroom. For me, the expense of paint seemed a bit superfluous. But trusting his lead paid dividends. He suggested a soft shade of golden yellow, and every morning thereafter I woke wrapped in sunlight.

I think about the places that have felt most like home whenever I read Genesis or Revelation. There's an arc between these two bookends. God creates a beautiful garden where he places Adam and Eve, and the apostle John tells us that one day God will make a new place for us, a heavenly city where we can dwell together forever. In the new Jerusalem, God is more than a divine landscape designer or interior decorator or general contractor. Instead, he operates more like a homemaker. What separates the homemaker from each of these artisans is where they go after the job is done. A homemaker continues to dwell in the space she has made. Her choices reflect the people who will share the home. She is strategically focused on their flourishing.

Among the similarities between the Garden of Eden and the new Jerusalem, the most brilliant is the presence of God. John describes the new Jerusalem as a place of unending light. God reveals the structural plan—a large, perfect square that evokes Solomon's temple—and he includes design elements that nod to Eden, the twelve tribes of Israel, and the apostles of Jesus. The city is heavily adorned in a multitude of jewels, with pearls large enough to act as gates and gold in every direction. No longer is the Word of God merely a lamp unto our feet, but the very presence of Jesus, the Word made flesh, shines throughout the city. And if I thought my subtle golden bedroom reflected sunlight stunningly, it cannot hold a candle to the interplay of God's radiance on all those faceted surfaces.

God our Father doesn't construct Eden and then leave us to fend for ourselves. He is more than the brilliant jeweler setting a gemstone foundation. He communes in the spaces he has formed. He is making a home, filling it with his incomparable light, and we are the family invited to dwell.

REFLECT   What images of Eden or from Revelation are most compelling to you? How might the image of God as a homemaker influence the way you manage your household?

PRAISE   Take some time to rejoice today that God dwells with us.

Floating Fortresses

God Makes a Home for Us

READ   Psalm 84:1–4

The waterbed I inherited in high school was a relic of my parents' that they unfortunately found would no longer support their aging backs. This bed was perfection, not only because I loved everything aquatic—I was basically a fish in the summers, sneaking through an unkempt bamboo forest to my grandparents' pool every day—but also because my frigid feet delighted to slip between preheated sheets as soon as the weather dropped below 70 degrees. My waterbed and I had our ups and downs. We had to snake the garden hose through the window to top her off every now and then. Once I accidentally missed my pincushion while sewing and pierced right through the plastic casing of the mattress. But most of the time, I took good care of this vintage artifact, and she took good care of me, cradling me each night as I quite literally floated off to sleep.

The first time God shared a home design with humans, it too floated on water. But in the case of Noah, water wasn't a warm and cozy friend; it was a tool for destruction, obliterating the evil that had populated God's good design. Noah's ark was a temporary home, but a protective fortress nonetheless. Generations later, God would preserve another of his followers in a micro ark, filled this time with a single guest instead of animals of every kind. Hidden in the reeds of the Nile River, the baby Moses was drawn out of the water by Pharaoh's daughter and graduated from a humble boathouse to a palace. Moses would have many homes over the course of his life as he led God's people through the wilderness to the edge of God's promised land.

We are used to thinking about fortresses on a hill, carved into the face of a rock and reinforced with spiked gates, moats, and shrewd marksmen on guard. Or grand palaces with high walls and finely dressed soldiers guarding the door. But the Lord of Armies is able to create a fortress out of humbler matter— gopherwood, papyrus, asphalt, pitch. He guards his people through desert wanderings and meets with them in tents. The security of these dwellings isn't found in the materials they are made of, but in the homemaker presiding over them.

Our homes today also come in many shapes and sizes. In love, we do our best to make them feel safe and comfortable, knowing that our family's health depends on much more than a good roof or our latest impulse buy at Ikea. Presence always outweighs presents. Study after study continues to affirm that quality, meaningful relationships in a family have a more powerful impact on a child's well-being than any specific contents inside a home.

God also prioritizes presence. He is constantly building a hedge of protection around those he loves, hiding us under the security of his wings, enveloping us in his steadfast care. This doesn't mean that we never experience hurt or sadness. What God allows or gives to us to bear is sometimes a mystery. Often in the Bible, God's protection does look like defeating armies in feats of masculine strength. But even when his protection doesn't come in the way we'd hoped, we can trust that he is always close and intimate, like the embrace of a mother who tucks her children safely into bed each night.

REFLECT As you consider how to create a protective home for your family, how does the Bible guide your priorities? How does Psalm 84 describe God's home?

PRAISE In what ways have you experienced God as a fortress?

The Home of a Womb

God Makes a Home for Us

READ   Genesis 12:1–3, 14:18–20, Luke 1:35–37, Genesis 1:2

Once every month, a healthy womb of a certain age tries to bring forth new life. An egg is released, signaling the uterine lining to thicken in preparation to receive the earliest beginnings of a growing baby. For nine months, a mother's body is also her baby's home.

When God told Adam and Eve to be fruitful and multiply, he assigned a task that would require them both. The man gives the seed and the woman an egg, but Eve's body provides more in this partnership than half the genetic material. Only she is designed to house the growing child. A woman offers a warm, sustaining home until her baby is strong enough to reside elsewhere.

When God chooses Abraham to be the father of the nation of Israel, the first command he gives is for Abraham to leave his old home and journey to a new one. Along his way, Abraham meets the priest Melchizedek, who blesses Abraham in the name of "God Most High, Creator of heaven and earth," using the same Hebrew word that we read in the passages about Eve and Lady Wisdom in entry 11. *Creator* is birthing language.[21]

In the beginning, God births the world into being, and now he will birth a new nation through the once-barren womb of Sarah. He makes a home for Israel inside a woman who lived her whole life unable to conceive. Then, God draws Israel out, calling them from their first home to follow him to a new one where they too will join in the work of the Garden, housing and bringing forth new life. A cycle, repeating again and again until Jesus.

The great disruption to the suffering of humanity made his first earthly home in the womb of a young girl, Mary of Nazareth. This was an impregnation like no other in all of history. While many ancient tales describe gods conceiving children with humans, Jesus was born of a virgin, created without a human father and without the typical human mechanics. In trying to imagine Mary's pregnancy through the lens of our modern scientific understanding, we might conclude that God supplied the male DNA needed to conceive Jesus, but the way Luke describes the encounter is deliberately nonsexual. The Spirit of God hovers over Mary just as he hovered over the waters at the dawn of creation in Genesis, just as the mother bird hovers over her nest.[22] By describing himself with feminine birthing language in Genesis, Proverbs, and beyond, God defies our human pattern of male plus female in the way he creates life. Yet he still brings Jesus into the world through the womb of Mary, just like Sarah and Eve and all the other women before her.

God honors the goodness of women's bodies. He brings life out of them, changing the shape of human history through his chosen people and entering into it from the home of a womb. This kind of homemaking is always blessed, and not only for those in the line of Christ. When our own wombs conceive, we make a new home for a new generation that will go out in their own way and change the world.

REFLECT   Consider how often the word "blessed" is used in the passages for today's reading. In what ways were these births a blessing specifically for the women who housed them? How are all Christian mothers invited into this blessing?

PRAISE   How has your baby been a blessing in your home?

Your Body Is a Temple

God Makes a Home for Us

READ   Psalm 27:4–10, Song of Songs 4:12–15,
1 Corinthians 6:18–20, Ephesians 5:31–33

Those who have ever repeated the mantra, "My body is a temple," as motivation to reject that extra bite, slip into running shoes, or kick some other harmful habit, may not realize that the apostle Paul uses this metaphor in a discussion of sexual purity that goes much deeper than general health advice. His assertion draws on imagery throughout Scripture about Israel's faithfulness to God and requires that we understand the centrality of their Temple for worship.

Before the sacrifice of Jesus, very few people could enjoy God in close quarters. King Solomon built a beautiful temple to be God's home, and the priests who entered this space were fortunate indeed. The design was a full-bodied experience, drawing its inhabitants to meditate on God through architecture and craftsmanship, engaging sight, touch, and smell. Fruit motifs and cherubim reminded worshippers of Eden, as lampstands' gold-leafed arms reached heavenward like the Tree of Life. The aroma from incense and oils inspired delight and evoked the future city of Delight,[23] where we will all one day be restored. God provided Solomon with highly specific instructions for making this home because he wanted those within it to be reminded of him.

Once a year, the High Priest was allowed to enter the very center of the Temple, into an area called the Holy of Holies where he would engage with God's presence directly. The Law of Moses detailed ritual sacrifice that would allow Israel's representatives to draw near to God's holiness without harm. Year after year, faithful Israelites brought offerings to the priests at regular intervals because this closeness required constant cleansing. Then one year, on a hill called Golgotha, God sacrificed his own son, an offering so pure and perfect and complete that we would never need cleansing again. The curtain that blocked the Holy of Holies was torn in two, and we were invited to dwell in God's home forever as the bride of Christ.

When Paul calls our body a temple and the church a bride, he points us to symbolism that culminates together in the Song of Songs. This poetic book describes a beloved bride with rich imagery from both the Garden of Eden and Solomon's Temple—choicest fruits, the aroma of sacrificial oils, and more. The bridegroom in these poems longs for more than a home with his bride; he yearns for perfect union. He describes her body like a holy place, and her womb is the Holy of Holies, a wellspring of life, where he is eager to dwell.[24]

God designed women's bodies to be a kind of home for our babies, and in the simplest way, we reflect God's care when we make this temple a safe dwelling place for them. But our bodies also tell the story of Christ united to his church. Into the most intimate part of ourselves, we invite our husband, and out of this space our children are born. When marital union results in new life, we present a picture of what happened when God came to dwell within us. His presence in us generates new life. Like the psalmist, we longed to draw near to him, but he instead came down to us. Our body is now a new kind of temple, a home where God is pleased to dwell, a home where life springs eternal.

REFLECT How does the temple imagery in the Bible impact your understanding of the Holy Spirit dwelling within you? What does the space you have made for your baby communicate to her about her identity and what your family values?

PRAISE As you read the passage from Psalm 27, thank God that he promises we will find him when we seek his face.

Well Done, Women

God Makes a Home for Us

"Our 20,000-year odyssey has shown women working under a variety of conditions. Their social status and economic production have varied together, reaching the lowest ebb when people valued least the contributions that women could make while rearing children."

—*Elizabeth Wayland Barber*[25]

READ   1 Timothy 4:7–8, Matthew 25:23

I cried when I first viewed the Egyptian collection in the Metropolitan Museum of Art in New York. I walked around cases of beads and burial objects, turned a corner and nearly ran into a glass cabinet with a fully intact headscarf. I got as close as nearby security guards would allow in order to examine the weaving pattern and marvel at what probably appeared to be a scrap of used bandages to others. But my mind was back in my Introduction to Costume Design class, where the professor explained that we can only guess at garment construction based on drawings from the Egyptians and those civilizations preceding them, since we have almost no preserved clothing from that period.

In the early days of archaeology, which has itself only taken off as a scientific field of study in the last century or so, most practitioners threw away fabrics in favor of the statuettes and tools wrapped inside them. Items like clothing and string-based tools were often lost to history because they disintegrated over time or weren't valued when they were found. Since these items were some of the only proof of women's work, we have long underestimated the powerful force that women's quiet contributions made.[26]

God designed us to make our homes in partnership. Most of our household chores today do not exclusively require a male or female body to complete them, so we have flexibility to collaborate with a spouse in the practical application of managing our households well. Anyone can make food and clothing or keep a shelter warm and tidy, but for most of human history, this work has fallen to women because it paired nicely with their unique childbearing role. While all members of a household would contribute to the family's flourishing in one way or another, young mothers could more easily grind grain, spin, and weave with children at their feet, while men went out into the fields or on a hunt. By this logic, labor divisions in antiquity were not a means to reduce women to lesser work but a way to elevate and make space for the good work of raising children.[27] Rather than drawing walls around what women could or could not do, this era asked a different question: what kind of work aligns with a woman's natural inclinations without hindering her ability to birth, nurse, and nurture her young family? Homemaking harnesses a woman's skills to create the context for her family to flourish. This is the work God is doing as he builds his church. He makes a home for us.

No matter what kind of work you do, paid or unpaid, in your physical home or elsewhere, God desires faithfulness. He gives each of us a unique set of skills and circumstances and cares more about how we steward what we have than who produces the most impressive final product. The question we should ask ourselves, now that we can buy a scarf at Target instead of harvesting, spinning, and weaving it, is how to work in a way that facilitates a healthy home. God's character, priorities, and wisdom are our homemaking guide, leading us to good work indeed.

REFLECT   How does Scripture inform your household priorities? How does the work you do, either inside or outside of the home, support your family's flourishing?

PRAISE   Consider how God's faithfulness to you might inspire your own faithfulness.

Restoring Our Home
God Makes a Home for Us

READ   John 14:23, Matthew 7:24–27, Titus 3:4–8, Hosea 6:6

During one of those summers where the heat crept in, we ate underneath a view of attic rafters. In a true act of God, our family was able to slip into the housing market by buying a small craftsman that teetered the knife's edge between a fixer-upper and a teardown. It was too nice for a real estate developer to flip for profit but had too many problems for the typical buyer. Room by room, we ripped out tile, drywall, and electrical wires, replacing them with materials that wouldn't burn the house down. We addressed the foundation and a cracked pipe that emptied the children's bathwater every night into a pool under our living room. And by "we" I mean mostly my husband.

Throughout our repairs, the goal remained the same. We wanted to restore the home to the safe and lovely space it was originally intended to be. We removed the brokenness and made the space whole again. Our choices, though limited by time, energy, and funds, were also thoughtful and strategic. We custom routed new trim to match the original and selected tile to complement what the first builders installed. We weren't trying to disguise our home as new construction, out with the old and in with everything "white and bright." Our choices were distinct because we were aiming to restore what once was.

Restoration is a throughline in the Bible. God built a wonderful home, but it fell into disrepair. Adam and Eve were invited to guard and cultivate the garden, but they wanted to be in charge of the whole project, thinking they could do it better their own way. And they failed, because they were never designed to call the shots. God called new representatives—Noah, Abraham and Sarah, then prophets, judges, and kings—each tasked to work toward this renovation. Some of God's representatives had to do a lot of demo work, clearing out idols in the temple and calling the people to repentance. Each added their own fingerprints to the project like children's hands in freshly poured concrete.

When Jesus came into the world, it wasn't to tear down the structures of the Law but to fulfill them. It was not "goodbye angry God, hello peace-and-love Jesus." Instead, God demonstrated how his way of living has always led to peace, hope, and a future. Jesus elevated the traditions of the nation of Israel, helping us to see what the Law was always meant to show. We will never be perfect by our own efforts.

Jesus was building more than a house, though. He was building a family, lifting women out of the shadows of society and welcoming them as sisters, inviting non-Jewish followers into the fold, bringing dignity to the outcast—all values that were part of the blueprint of the Law that had been lost or corrupted over time. But most importantly, Jesus promised to make his home within each of us and with the church collectively.

As walking, talking houses of worship, indwelled with the Holy Spirit, we also are called to join the restoration. Sometimes this will entail quite a bit of demolition—removing old ideas that do not align with Scripture and letting go of habits that draw us away from God. As we rearrange the structures of our lives, our eyes must stay fixed on Jesus. We build on the solid foundation of the Rock of Ages and make sure every board and brick declares his praise.

REFLECT In the rain and winds of family life, how is your spiritual "house" holding up? As you consider ways that your life is structured, what areas might need some restoration? What does Titus teach us about God's involvement in our good works?

PRAISE Consider Hosea 6:6. How does this passage provide hope when you are tempted to fix up your life by your own efforts?

Mansions in Heaven

God Makes a Home for Us

READ   John 14:1–7

The first time I went to a home of some wealth, I almost didn't notice. I was gathering with colleagues for a post-event recap. Our host Karis[28] lived in one of the hilly neighborhoods in Los Angeles where front doors are unassuming, but open into multilevel residences built into the hillside. In her entryway, I glimpsed a painting in the style of the pop artist Roy Lichtenstein. I'm not much of a modern art fan myself, so I felt particularly cultured to make such an observation. We gathered in a modestly sized kitchen over brunch, where Karis graciously greeted each person as they arrived. Nothing about her space felt showy, and the warmth of our casual conversation distracted me from some of the finer details in her home. Karis was a captivating presence. When we moved our meeting down to the recessed living room, I noticed other paintings, including one which filled the entire high-ceilinged wall. My office mate shot me a discreetly raised eyebrow and gestured to this piece with her chin, reminding me of a conversation we had at the start of the project. Karis was an art collector, and that was a real Lichtenstein.

It's tempting to be attracted to wealth for what it can supply you. I've seen this cycle play out more times than I can count—parents arranging playdates with families of similar status, or an executive politely excusing herself from a conversation once she realizes the other person offers no networking value. If we are honest, we sometimes treat God this way as well. We desire peaceful lives, well-behaved children, and good mental health. Heaven sounds like a nice place to go when life is over. So we might attend church and read our Bible hoping for some kind of transactional blessing. If

I hang around with the right kind of Christians, maybe some of their spiritual wealth will rub off on me.

On the night he was betrayed, Jesus promised to go and prepare a place for his disciples in his Father's house. The King James version of the Bible translated his description of God's home as one filled with "many mansions," giving some readers Beverly Hills vibes—as if the beauty of God's promise lies in manicured lawns that lead to majestic arched entrance halls and a customized collection of amenities at our service. But Jesus's words evoke the marriage customs of the day and the ultimate union between Christ and his church. His emphasis is not on the home construction itself. When a husband prepares a new home for his bride, the details of the rooms matter only inasmuch as they serve the new family. The one who invites you to dwell with him matters more than the dwelling itself.

God doesn't mind mixing metaphors. In fact, he regularly utilizes them in combination to communicate his indescribable nature in a framework that we might understand. The Bible calls the church the bride of Christ and welcomes her to make a home with him. Jesus is both the husband in this word picture and also God the Father. In the perfection of his triune nature, God is similar to both an exquisite lover and a nurturing parent. If earthly blessings from God are more attractive to us than he is, this is because we do not fully comprehend all that his presence has to offer.

Our humble attempts at encapsulating beauty with oil and canvas testify to God's creative power residing within us. Maybe our homes in heaven will be adorned with all the best that the human art world can afford. But it won't be the first thing we notice. Because God's presence will captivate our whole selves.

REFLECT What does the passage from John's gospel teach us about God? How does this vision of our future home impact the way you make your home today?

PRAISE What aspects of God's character captivate you?

part 06

God Grows a Family

God's deliverance, nourishment, nurturing, and homemaking inspires not only our biological mothering but also how we relate together with other believers as the family of God. Where we see evidence of God's character in our own mothering or in the lives of friends, God invites us to marvel that these beautiful reflections are only a whisper of his ultimate mothering care. The church is a family where we grow into motherhood together.

DATE: / /	BABY IS:	weeks | months old
I FEEL...		

Mothers in Scripture

God Grows a Family

READ   Ruth 4:13–17, Luke 10:38–42, 2 Timothy 1:5, 3:14–17

You can learn more about the women from today's reading in the following passages:
Deborah - Judges 4–5
Tamar - Genesis 38
Abigail - 1 Samuel 25
Hannah - 1 Samuel 1–2
Bathsheba - 2 Samuel 11–12, 1 Kings 1:11–31

God bless the oversharer. As much as I can appreciate the value of healthy boundaries in relationships, I am thankful for people in my life who are willing to get deep when we have a few moments to connect. In a world where we are often isolated by either physical space or busy schedules, I am grateful to skip the small talk. My soul is hungry for connection, and another's willingness to be vulnerable allows for meaningful conversation, even with our limited time.

Whenever I get to know new people, I listen to offhand comments like I'm skimming the chapter titles of a book. Was that a reference to diet culture? Did she just drop a hint that her childhood home looked a little like mine? When social convention allows, those are the chapters I dive into—the ones where we might have a deeper connection. This is also how I have learned to read the women in the Bible. Some of their stories offer hardly any details, and others preserve their exact words. In Scripture we see a whole range of women, young and old, married and single, in a variety of professions. If we listen closely to their stories, we learn more about ourselves and about God. We are invited to meditate on their experiences and compare and contrast them with God's mother-like care and our own.

So we consider Deborah, who calls herself a "Mother in Israel" even though she held official titles as their judge and tactical military leader. She shepherds God's people in a more public way than Ruth, the faithful daughter-in-law, who risked a midnight visit to ask Boaz to provide permanently for her family. Ruth acts shrewdly to encourage the men in the town to uphold the levirate marriage responsibility, although she doesn't have nearly as difficult a time doing so as Tamar did with her father-in-law, Judah. Both would become mothers in the genealogy of Christ, bearing witness to the kind of women who are welcome in the family of God. A few generations down the line, Abigail also skirts disaster through wise action, and Mary of Bethany sits at the feet of Jesus, soaking up the source of wisdom himself. They demonstrate how to follow God, while Hannah foreshadows God's work more directly, giving her beloved son to service in the temple, just as God would one day give his own Son as our perfect Priest.

These women passed their wisdom down through the generations—joined by Bathsheba, who raised a young Solomon before he was known as the wisest of kings, and Lois and Eunice, who invested in the spiritual development of Paul's protégé Timothy. We too are called to raise our children to know the Lord and walk in his ways. Many mothers in Scripture reflect God's care for his children. They are made in his image, each reflecting him in her own mirror fragment, and invite us to join their legacy. Together, we make the image more complete. For we are the mothers of the church God is building, and in ways big and small, we will leave our impressions just as they have.

REFLECT When you think about the legacy of women before you, who could be considered part of your genealogy in a spiritual sense? How do the women in Scripture inform your understanding of God's deliverance, nourishment, nurturing, and homemaking? What mothering traits do you hope to pass along to the next generation?

PRAISE How has God used Scripture to train you in righteousness?

Doulas Among Us

God Grows a Family

READ   1 Corinthians 3:1–9, Luke 1:38

If my first labor had progressed with the calm of the prenatal yoga class I took beforehand, I might have had an accidental home birth. When I signed up, I was expecting some kind of augmented stretching course that took my widening middle into account, but this instructor was really a birth coach. She focused our time on supported resting poses that were intended to relax the body during labor. Each Tuesday, I ambled past an Indian food restaurant into the dim studio and collected a mat, bolster, blocks, and forty or so blankets. Setting the props for each posture took several minutes, but once the instructor adjusted all the blankets and rolled my shoulders just right, there was a 50/50 chance I'd immediately fall asleep. I assume that those who hired this yoga teacher as a doula received such thoughtful and attentive birthing support that their babies arrived peacefully, with no more effort than a deep sigh.

Perhaps my fantasy of birth support isn't a far cry from what it could have looked like before Eve listened to the serpent and ate the fruit, but now we live in a fallen, broken place where no perfect poses can completely erase the pain of bringing children into the world. Out of this mess of humanity, God promises to deliver us. Here also we find a room full of spiritual sisters supporting our labor like the hands and feet of Jesus himself.

Certainly, fathers and brothers play an important role for the full family of God to grow, but the influence of women in our communities cannot be overstated. Those who have experienced similar labor to our own can often speak into the most personal spaces of our hearts. They are able to recognize our struggles and sin when we are in the throes of pain and offer recommendations for how to turn and push differently.

We considered earlier how the apostle Paul used nurturing language in his letter to the Thessalonians. He employs similar metaphors when describing the work of building the Corinthian church. Though he established the church, other significant spiritual influences, like Apollos and Cephas, invested in its growth. Eventually the community began to divide along party lines, each claiming that they were following the "best" leader. Paul admonishes this tribalism by emphasizing the teamwork needed for both harvest and building, two analogies that help us understand how God grows a family. In the field, one sows and another waters, but Christ gives the growth. On the construction site, each builds upon Christ the foundation, and their work is either unified in quality or is burned by the fire. If we apply the language of labor to Paul's argument, we see in the church a community of doulas, some offering support during spiritual labor, others providing food and cleaning postpartum. We are night nurses keeping watch and wet nurses stepping in to feed when something goes awry.

I marvel that God would invite others to join the labor, and yet this is the clear message of Scripture. When the angel Gabriel tells Mary that God has chosen her to be the mother of Jesus, she responds in glad affirmation, calling herself the Lord's servant. The Greek word she uses, *doulē*, is where we get the word doula.[29] She is both the mother of God's son and also the doula who assists God in his plan to bring eternal life to all who would follow Jesus.

Like Mary, we are all servants in God's work. We reflect his nature through our collective strength, but none of us bears the full burden alone. God safely brings new life into the world, and our role is to plant and cultivate. So we spiritually nurse and nurture one another faithfully, nesting as we make our homes into fertile soil.

REFLECT   Who are the spiritual doulas co-laboring in your community? Where might you need to reach out for support? Who might God be calling you to help?

PRAISE   How has God given your baby growth in recent weeks?

Waiting for Redemption

God Grows a Family

READ   Romans 8:18–27, 5:1–5

Prodromal labor is a term I wish I'd known during the languishing days in late summer of 2014. I was skittish from all the stories about fast second labors, so I told my boss that baby number two was on his way at the first sign of steady contractions. I took a long bath. We alerted the circle of friends who had promised to look after our toddler, and I settled into my bed expecting to wake in active labor sometime in the night.

But the sun rose once again, and all was quiet. My bouncing boy performed his usual morning stretches and somersaults, but my uterus had presumably clocked out for the night. Perplexed and disappointed, I commenced my own routine, which at some point convinced my belly to look alert and get a move on. Labor began again. And then stopped. Began. Stopped. Began. Stopped. And I waited.

Mothering has involved a lot more waiting than I would have liked. Waiting for two blue lines. Waiting for clumsy fingers to fiddle socks onto fat toddler feet. Waiting for the test results, for the medicine to kick in, for the chatter to cease. Waiting for the right time to push.

But while we have been incubating new life, creation along with us is waiting for the perfection of Eden to be restored. Pregnancy, at its best, is a beautiful picture of what it feels like to eagerly wait for our wildest dream to finally arrive. We wait through the nausea, swelling, and round ligament pain. We breathe through heartburn, doubt, and contractions. Challenges rise to a fever pitch, and we long to be set free from the difficulty of it all.

If you've experienced labor, then you know a little bit about what Paul is trying to describe to the church in Rome. He tells them that the whole earth is groaning as if in the pains of labor. The suffering is fierce and stretched out as if it may never end, but it is also purposeful. As the pain increases, we all get closer to the glory that is about to be revealed.

In this way, birthing a child teaches us what the whole earth has experienced since the ground of the Garden was cursed. All of God's good creation, in its broken and fallen state, is also waiting for a Son. This is Jesus—the child whose birth means more than the end to our pregnancy woes. A child whose life brings life unimaginable.

Even as we experience God's mothering care, delivering us from sin which so easily entangles and nourishing us through his Word and our spiritual community, our redemption is still in process. Just as these different mothering images give us merely part of the picture of what God is like, we only ingest them in small, incomplete doses this side of eternity. They, like a long, stop-and-start labor, point us forward to our full and perfect home, where someday we will dwell in God's nurturing presence forever.

REFLECT How does the depth of your own groanings in pregnancy and labor illuminate what Paul writes in his letter to the Romans? In what ways do you find yourself waiting today? How does our future hope impact your willingness to persevere through trials?

PRAISE Thank God for specific ways he has been training you in endurance.

The Hope of Mothering

God Grows a Family

READ   Romans 8:28–30, 2 Corinthians 4:16–18,
Hebrews 4:14–16

In labor, birthing instructors will remind you that pain is productive. Most of the time, when our bodies experience discomfort, pain is a warning signal to indicate that something is wrong. But during childbirth, the stronger a mother's contractions become, the closer she is to delivery. You are encouraged to relax into the intensity of labor and welcome the ebb and flow of pain as a sign that you are about to meet your baby. Staying calm in the midst of labor pain requires focused attention because welcoming this kind of suffering is counterintuitive. Even if we can trust that our bodily pain will lead to new life, we cannot ignore sin's curse—our multiplied sorrow in childbearing is very present in the delivery room.

Birth does a number on our bodies, and the expectation that we must quickly return to our pre-baby physique is no friend in the process. Paul's words in his second letter to the Corinthians never felt more true for me than after I had a couple of kids. Whether it's additional weight, stretch marks, or a blown-out pelvic floor, our postpartum bodies often feel like they are being destroyed. If I'm being honest, it doesn't always feel like a "light, momentary affliction."

If your changing body doesn't get you down, worries about your children certainly will. God does not give guarantees for their health or safety. Our children will get sick and hurt, sometimes with permanent disabilities. Friends will betray them. Their hard work may amount to disappointing outcomes. We may faithfully teach the Bible, and they could still stray from the faith.

So given all of this sorrow, why would we choose to mother at all?

To invest your time and energy in a child is a radically hopeful task. Your work declares to the watching world that flourishing is still possible on this earth, no matter how sad or evil or fallen the world may be. We wake each day and do the work required of us—another load of laundry, another dirty diaper, another splat of puree on the floor—all the while, believing that God will transform our work into something good. Mothering is inherently hopeful because it does not allow us to resign ourselves to death. Mothering chooses life.

But even if we enter into motherhood with the purest hope, the days are long and discouragement is sure to come. When I don't feel up to the task, I am reminded that God always finishes the good work that he started. He is still transforming you just like he's still working on me, and he won't stop until we look just like him. We can persevere in our mothering even when it wrecks our bodies and hearts because we have a mothering God in heaven who can relate to our struggles. He offers the wisdom, patience, and love we so desperately need.

REFLECT What are your radical hopes for your baby? What challenges or "productive pain" are you facing that you long to see God work out for good? How is God renewing your inner person?

PRAISE How do the diverse facets of God's mothering presence give you hope?

The Church Is a Birthing Room
God Grows a Family

READ   2 Corinthians 12:9–10, Philippians 2:3–11

Childbirth is one of the defining capacities of the female body. Not every woman will experience it, but no man ever will. I am struck by how God designed birth to be both uniquely strong and also radically vulnerable. Bearing children requires incredible fortitude and might. The physical process takes grit and full-body commitment. At the same time, it highlights our need for a complementing partner, our need for support outside of ourselves. Back in the days when women birthed in the wilderness, it was advantageous to have a relatively larger male nearby to protect the space and kick away an opportunistic wolf. But even in labor today, with all its hospital sterility and medical advances, a father's support is invaluable. A laboring woman is both ferocious and also exposed.

During the physical strain of pregnancy and the duress of labor, a good father commits to support his wife with more than a paycheck or sturdy hand to hold. He arranges their life together to ensure that she is well nourished and rested. He tends to her physical needs after her body is torn by vaginal delivery or stitched up from a cesarean. He invests spiritually in both their relationship together and in their kids. He is a listening ear, slow to speak, but ready with truth when she needs to hear it. The security that comes from knowing that your child's father will not abandon you to do the immense work of parenting alone provides an emotional well-being that we should not take for granted. As many women (perhaps yourself included) can sadly confirm, the absence of a good father is deeply felt. And that is not how God intended motherhood to be.

When my third baby was born, my husband made the kind of observation that is only possible when it's not your first rodeo. In the final moments of pushing, amid his cheers and snapping camera, he suddenly felt an acute contrast between his presence as the only male in the room and the energy of my nurses and doctor. The women gave me specific directions—micro adjustments to my positioning, guidance for where to focus each push, and confident assurance that my son was almost here. Here he saw women doing what women do best, providing me with expert instruction, delivered in the uniquely feminine way that I most needed in that moment.

My husband was a blessing in that room. I needed him as the father of our baby to arrange this moment for my safety, to feel him guarding and protecting me in my vulnerability, and to know that he would stick around to support us all in his unique fatherly way.

But I also needed some mothers.

The remarkable ability to bear a child is a superpower we are not designed to wield alone. This great strength of ours requires us to acknowledge our humble vulnerability. Fathers and brothers have gifts that enrich our families in ways specific to men, while mothers and sisters surround us with wisdom, nourishing and nurturing us as we make a home for our growing child. Our hope in the family of God—whether or not we have husbands or brothers or sisters in a literal sense—springs up from the good news of Jesus's resurrection, and its fruit is our communion. We are made new and united.

Birth gives us a picture of how the family of God is meant to operate, as we each reflect different aspects of God's mothering and fathering care. In a way, the church should feel like a birthing room, where both men and women bring our gifts to the table together, working in unity to bring forth new life.

REFLECT   What have you learned about mothering that you can offer to the church? How is God at work in your vulnerability? How does Christ's servanthood inspire you to serve others?

PRAISE   How has God's mothering care influenced your own mothering?

Ready for Life

I've worn this tent dress
once a week
for the last month
and it's as threadbare as I feel
—stretched—
to house rambunctious life.

Every day I wake in
wonder
perhaps the last day
I ever carry a child.
The last rhythmic hiccups.
Last bump picture.
Last tiny feet tracing
secret messages on my left side belly.

Can I burn these memories securely in my mind?

*Will all I've learned and studied and applied in this season
be doomed to slowly fade with age?*

*Does wisdom hang onto our formative moments for later recall
or is everything given then gone, for such a time as this?*

How do you capture a pregnancy,
a graduation,
a first kiss,
a last breath?

For we are dust
stardust
leaving a trail behind
as we blaze into eternity.

Acknowledgements

My eyes were first opened to the images of God as a laboring woman, midwife, and breastfeeding mother by the work of Lauren Winner, and I am deeply grateful to the foundation her writing laid in my own study and meditation. She is not the first to reflect on these ideas, nor my only influence, and I have done my best to cite all who enhanced my reflections. I owe a deep debt to my community of spiritual mothers—the ones I know personally and women whose work I have read over the years. Their collective impact is interwoven in this book. These words are my humble contribution to a conversation that I hope will continue to season and ripen with age.

This particular labor of love was delivered thanks to the gorgeous design of Whitney Farnsworth, editing by Amy Carbo, insights from early readers—Brian, Rebekah, Camille, and Alyssa—and the cheers and breath coaching of my dearest Phil.

Endnotes

1. Herman Bavinck, *The Wonderful Works of God: Instruction in the Christian Religion According to the Reformed Confession* (Glenside, PA: Westminster Seminary, 2019), 116.

2. "Purple Cauliflower," *Specialty Produce*, accessed July 18, 2022, https://specialtyproduce.com/produce/Purple_Cauliflower_1122.php.

3. Kathleen Norris, *The Quotidian Mysteries: Laundry, Liturgy, and "Women's Work"* (New York/Mahwah, NJ: Paulist, 1998), 10.

4. The Editors of Encyclopedia Britannica, "Doldrums," *Encyclopedia Britannica*, July 20, 1998, https://www.britannica.com/science/doldrums.

5. Tracee Cornforth, "The Endometrium and Its Role in Reproductive Health: Periods, Pregnancy, and Potential Problems," *Verywell Health*, last modified April 13, 2023, https://www.verywellhealth.com/what-is-the-endometrium-2721857.

6. Lauren F. Winner, *Wearing God: Clothing, Laughter, Fire, and Other Overlooked Ways of Meeting God* (New York: Harper Collins, 2015), 152.

7. Isaiah 42:14, ESV

8. Amy E. Marga, "What Motherly Images for God are in the Bible?" *Enter the Bible*, last modified September 17, 2021, https://enterthebible.org/what-motherly-images-for-god-are-in-the-bible-amy-e-marga.

9. Marga, "What Motherly Images for God are in the Bible?"

10. Cahleen Shrier, "The Science of the Crucifixion," adapted by Tally Flint, *Azusa Pacific University*, March 1, 2002, https://www.apu.edu/articles/the-science-of-the-crucifixion.

11. J. David Cassel, "Defending the Cannibals," *Christianity Today*, January 1, 1998, https://www.christianitytoday.com/history/issues/issue-57/defending-cannibals.html.

12. Tars Jan van Bavel, "Maternal Aspects in Salvation History According to Augustine," *Augustiniana* 47, no. 3/4 (January 1997), 258. https://www.jstor.org/stable/44992644

13. Patti Carroll, "You Are What You Eat . . . and So Is Your Baby," *Centers for Disease Control and Prevention*, July 31, 2017, https://blogs.cdc.gov/publichealthmatters/2017/07/you-are-what-you-eatand-so-is-your-baby/.

14. Jon Collins, Tim Mackie, and Carissa Quinn, "The Womb of God? - Character of God E3," August 31, 2020, in *Character of God*, produced by BibleProject, podcast, 00:21:00, https://bibleproject.com/podcast/the-womb-of-god/.

15. Carissa Quinn, "God is Like a Nursing Mother," *BibleProject*, accessed November 27, 2022, https://bibleproject.com/blog/god-is-like-a-nursing-mother/.

16. Van Bavel, "Maternal Aspects," 283.

17. Catherine Caruso, "Pregnancy Causes Lasting Changes in a Woman's Brain," *Scientific American*, December 19, 2016, https://www.scientificamerican.com/article/pregnancy-causes-lasting-changes-in-a-womans-brain/.

18. Alexandra Sacks, "Matrescence: The Developmental Transition to Motherhood," *Psychology Today*, April 8, 2019, https://www.psychologytoday.com/us/blog/motherhood-unfiltered/201904/matrescence-the-developmental-transition-to-motherhood.

19. "'Refuge' in the Psalms," *BibleMesh*, March 4, 2014, https://biblemesh.com/blog/refuge-in-the-psalms/.

20. Gene L. Green, *The Letters to the Thessalonians* (Grand Rapids, MI: Wm. B. Eerdmans, 2002), 127–128.

21. Marga, "What Motherly Images for God are in the Bible?"

22. Amy Peeler, *Women and the Gender of God* (Grand Rapids, MI: Wm. B. Eerdmans, 2022), 34.

23. See imagery of the New Jerusalem in Isaiah 62.

24. Aimee Byrd, *The Sexual Reformation: Restoring the Dignity and Personhood of Man and Woman* (Grand Rapids, MI: Zondervan Reflective, 2022), 54–55, 63.

25. Elizabeth Wayland Barber, *Women's Work: The First 20,000 Years—Women, Cloth, and Society in Early Times* (New York, NY: W. W. Norton,1994), 283.

26. Barber, *Women's Work*, 286–287.

27. Judith K. Brown, "A Note on the Division of Labor by Sex," *American Anthropologist* 72, no. 5 (October 1970), 1075–1076. https://www.jstor.org/stable/671420.

28. Some details in this story have been altered for privacy.

29. "Doula," *Online Etymology Dictionary*, accessed December 28, 2022, https://www.etymonline.com/word/doula.

About the Author

Meredith Storrs works in educational administration, despite a degree in costume design. During her college years at USC, she swapped the summer thunderstorms of Texas for the roar of the Pacific Ocean, where she grew her passion for storytelling both onstage and behind the scenes. Meredith is a huge nerd for all things theology and enjoys translating heady ideas and academic-speak into everyday language to help people see the depth and beauty of the Bible. She serves her local church as a lay teacher, writer, and editor. When the stars align, she still sews. Meredith lives in the heart of Los Angeles (on purpose) with her husband and three kids.

www.meredithstorrs.com
Instagram: @meredithstorrs
Twitter: @meredith_storrs

Made in the USA
Las Vegas, NV
15 June 2023

73469353R00059